CREC *and* CNIDE

ARTHUR AND HIS COURT HUNTING THE WHITE STAG.
(Paris, Bibliothèque Nationale, fonds français 1376, fol. 107.)

EREC and ENIDE

Chrétien de Troyes

TRANSLATED WITH
AN INTRODUCTION AND NOTES BY
DOROTHY GILBERT

UNIVERSITY OF CALIFORNIA PRESS

BERKELEY   LOS ANGELES   LONDON

University of California Press
Berkeley and Los Angeles, California

University of California Press, Ltd.
London, England

© 1992 by
The Regents of the University of California

Library of Congress Cataloging-in-Publication Data

Chrétien, de Troyes, 12th cent.
 [Erec et Enide. English]
 Erec and Enide / translated with an introduction and notes by
Dorothy Gilbert.
  p. cm.
 Translated from the Old French.
 Translation of: Erec et Enide / Chrétien de Troyes.
 Includes bibliographical references.
 ISBN 0-520-07345-2 (alk. paper). — ISBN 0-520-07346-0 (pbk.:
alk. paper)
 1. Erec (Legendary character)—Romances. 2. Arthurian romances.
I. Gilbert, Dorothy, 1936– . II. Title.
PQ1445.E6A34 1992
841'.1—dc20   91-43103
                                                              CIP

Printed in the United States of America
9 8 7 6 5 4 3 2

The paper used in this publication meets the minimum requirements of
American National Standard for Information Sciences—Permanence of Paper
for Printed Library Materials, ANSI Z39.48-1984. ∞

In memory of Genevieve H. Gilbert

CONTENTS

Acknowledgments   ix

Introduction   1

Suggestions for Further Reading   33

EREC AND ENIDE   39

Notes to the Poem   253

Glossary of Names and Places   265

ACKNOWLEDGMENTS

IT IS A GREAT SATISFACTION to express my thanks to the many people who have helped me with this book. First, the curators and staff of the Salle des Manuscrits at the Bibliothèque Nationale made it possible for me to examine the six more or less complete manuscripts of the original that are part of their collection and also granted permission to use the photograph of an illuminated page of MS 1376 (f. 107). The Musée Condé at Chantilly allowed me to examine the seventh manuscript (MS 472). Doe Library of the University of California at Berkeley also provided much essential material.

The National Endowment for the Humanities offered invaluable material and moral support in granting me a year's stipend to do research at Doe Library and write a large portion of the translation. I am particularly grateful for the warm personal enthusiasm shown by Susan A. Mango, formerly of the NEH, and by Mary T. Chunko, whose article describing my project, "Quest for *le mot juste*," appeared in the NEH journal *Humanities* (7, no. 3 [June 1986]). A later award enabled me to spend the summer of 1988 at the NEH Literary Translation Institute at the University of California at Santa Cruz. This was a rare and delightful opportunity for uninterrupted work and for congenial association with other translators. Gabriel Berns and Joanna Bankier, who ran the Institute, gave me much support and specific criticism; Maggie Collins saw most capably to my material needs.

The enthusiasm, faith, patience, and practical counsel of my editor at the University of California Press, Doris Kretschmer, have been beyond all price. Also invaluable was the astute and meticulous work of my copyeditor, Rose Vekony, who brought to this book not only her editorial skills but her thorough knowledge of Old French literature. Numerous scholars in the field of medieval literature have extended their support and shared their expert knowledge; thanks are due Joseph J. Duggan, Gerald Herman, Roger J. Steiner, E. Jane Burns, Roberta L. Krueger, and especially Charles Muscatine. Robert Harrison and William W. Kibler refereed the manuscript and gave extremely helpful suggestions; R. Howard Bloch read the Introduction and advised me on the body of scholarship and criticism of Chrétien's works, as did Susie Sutch. Jean H. Perkins and Anne Winters put their expertise in French texts and their literary acumen to the service of my translation, offering useful pointers. The late Peter Whigham, blessed as he was with a fine poetic ear and a great gift for teaching the difficult art of literary translation, contributed many hours of patient reading, thought, and advice. Sandra M. Gilbert's poetic ear, scholarly astuteness, and knowledgeable advice on many matters of manuscript preparation have been priceless benefits. I am grateful as well to the late Elliot Gilbert and to Roger Gilbert for their excellent advice. Others who have been generous with their support, their interest, their time, or their literary and scholarly judgment are Frederick Amory, Willis Barnstone, Alfred Bloom, Lina Brock, Susan M. Brown, Joan C. Carr, Marilyn Chandler, Frederick Fornoff, Avriel H. Goldberger, Robert J. Griffin, Edward Milowicki, James Monroe, David Parent, Daniel Silvia, Carolyn Tipton, and Albert Wachtel.

The gift of a computer by my brother, Charles E. Gilbert, made the task of preparing the manuscript infinitely easier; his patient tutelage and that of my nephew, Steven Curtin, and my friends Sandra and Elliot Gilbert greatly facilitated the appearance of this work. My immediate family has given me support and enthusiasm to a degree I can never repay. Much *caritas* has been extended to me in this labor, and that is now a source of joy and gratitude. Any errors that remain in this book are of course my own.

INTRODUCTION

THE FIRST KNOWN ARTHURIAN ROMANCE, *Erec and Enide* was com-
posed about 1170. Whether it had precursors is a subject of debate
and conjecture. As far as we know, Chrétien de Troyes created the
genre, drawing on ancient Celtic legend, classical and ecclesiastical
Latin learning, and the literary and social conventions of French
culture in his day. The twelfth century had already produced the
French epic, or chanson de geste, which celebrated the matter of
France (the deeds of Charlemagne and his warriors, and the epic
cycles of William and of the Rebel Barons) and the matter of Rome
(the deeds of heroes and princes of antiquity). In the previous
generation, romances had been created from classical material (the
Roman de Thèbes, the *Roman de Troie,* and the *Roman d'Eneas*); in
Chrétien's own time Béroul and Thomas created their romances of
Tristan. Also roughly contemporary with Chrétien was the distinguished Marie de France, whose *lais,* drawn from Breton tales and
songs and imbued with Celtic themes, often portray human limitation or cruelty that is exposed or remedied by fairies, changelings,
werewolves, or other supernatural beings. Such, in broad terms, was
the cultural climate that conditioned Chrétien and with which,
through his skill in creating a *bele conjointure,* [1] he suffused his
versatile and civilized art.

---

1. *Erec et Enide,* line 16. In his prologue, lines 1–28, Chrétien sets forth an
aesthetic of a well-constructed narrative, or "molt bele conjointure."

Erec and Enide is the first of five extant romances known to be the work of Chrétien. The others are *Cligès; Yvain,* or *The Knight with the Lion; Lancelot,* or *The Knight of the Cart;* and *Perceval, or the Story of the Grail.* The influence of these works on European literature has been enormous. In Chrétien's own time, or shortly thereafter, his works—notably *Perceval*—were continued, expanded, or cast into other versions. Robert de Boron, scholars are convinced, knew Chrétien's *Perceval;* Robert's ambition, however, was to write a trilogy of verse romances describing the whole history of the Grail and of Arthur's reign. Of this trilogy only the first part, *Joseph,* or *Le Roman de l'Estoire dou Graal,* and 502 lines of the second part, *Merlin,* survive in their original verse form, in a late thirteenth-century manuscript. These romances were soon worked into prose versions, which became popular and were in turn expanded and imitated. *Perlesvaus* appeared sometime between 1191 and 1250; it, with the work of Chrétien and Robert de Boron, gave rise to the voluminous cycle known as the Vulgate prose romances. One of these, *Lancelot,* is believed to be directly descended from Chrétien; others, written in the early thirteenth century and employing much Arthurian material familiar to modern readers, include the *Queste del Saint Graal,* the *Grand Saint Graal,* the *Mort Artu* (Malory's chief source), and the *Estoire de Merlin.* These works were immensely popular and were widely disseminated.

Outside of France Chrétien's influence extended to the Middle High German poets Hartmann von Aue (*Erec, Iwein*) and Wolfram von Eschenbach (*Parzifal*), who wrote one generation later; the Old Norse *Erexsaga* and *Ivensaga* (prose narratives) are still later versions of Chrétien romances. There is a Swedish version of Chrétien's *Yvain, Ivan Lejonsriddaren,* or "Ivan, the Knight of the Lion," a poem in rhymed couplets; the manuscript states that it was translated from the French in 1303. The fourteenth-century Middle

English poem *Ywain and Gawain* is a shorter version of Chrétien's *Yvain*. But these are only the most direct descendants. As the artist who first celebrated Arthurian chivalry in the romance genre, Chrétien opened the way for the Middle English romances, including the magnificent *Sir Gawain and the Green Knight,* and his influence extends ultimately to Chaucer, Malory, Spenser, Tennyson, and Robinson Jeffers, as well as to Richard Wagner—to mention only a few of the most illustrious participants in the tradition.

Lancelot is unfinished (Chrétien turned the tale over to a collaborator, Godefroi de Lagny), and *Perceval,* left incomplete at the poet's death, was continued by others. A sixth romance, *William of England,* is often attributed (with caution) to Chrétien. In his prologue to *Cligès* the poet claims to have written a version of the Tristan story, *King Marc and Iseut the Blond;* it may have been a romance or a short episode, but in any case it is lost. Two lyric poems, which show influence of the troubadours, are often attributed to him, and he claims authorship of four poems that are apparently versions of Ovid. Three of these, *Les Comandemanz Ovide* (Ovid's *Remedia amoris?*), *L'Art d'amors* (Ovid's *Ars amandi?*), and *Le Mors de l'espaule* (in English, *The Shoulder Bite*) do not survive. The surviving Ovidian poem, *La Muance de la hupe, de l'aronde et du rossignol* (*The Change of the Hoopoe, the Swallow, and the Nightingale,* better known as the *Philomena*), was preserved in a thirteenth-century *Ovid moralisé.* It is often conjectured that the Ovidiana were written before the romances and may have been apprentice work.

What little we know about Chrétien is based almost entirely on internal evidence (like the list of works in *Cligès*) and on our knowledge of his world. He flourished after 1164 until possibly as late as the 1190s at the court of Henry I of Champagne and his countess, Marie, the daughter of Eleanor of Aquitaine and Louis VII of France.[2] He dedicated his *Perceval* to Philip of Alsace, count of Flanders, at whose court he may have served before the count's departure for the Third Crusade in 1190 (Philip was killed at Acre the next year). Apart from this information, we are left with conjecture.

Gaston Paris, Jean Frappier, and others have speculated, not at all conclusively, about what role Chrétien played in his society, suggesting that he might have been a herald or a page, or was perhaps the Christianus, canon of Saint-Loup at Troyes, whose name is found in a charter of 1173. But was Chrétien an ecclesiastic? Frappier points out that Christianus was not a rare name in that age; he also believes that the poet expressed too worldly and secular a spirit for an ecclesiastic.[3]

This thought bears pondering, since Chrétien's age produced ecclesiastics whose outlook could appear noticeably worldly. A striking example is Andreas Capellanus (André the Chaplain), who also served at Marie's court (c. 1170–1180) and whose sophisticated, at times mordant Ovidian work *De amore* (often called *The Art of Courtly Love*) shows an extremely "mundane" perspective—Andreas's retraction notwithstanding—and one that is ethically far more relaxed than Chrétien's. For example, a large section of Andreas's work consists of dialogues that serve as recommended scripts for aspiring lovers of various social classes. There are scripts

    2. John F. Benton, in "The Court of Champagne as a Literary Center," *Speculum* 36 (1961): 553–54, maintains that Chrétien's chronology could begin five years earlier, if not more; he believes that Henry and Marie were betrothed as early as 1153 and could have married as early as 1159. Anthime Fourrier, in *Mélanges de langue et de littérature du moyen-âge et de la Renaissance offerts à Jean Frappier* (Geneva: Droz, 1970), 299–311, offers a rebuttal to Benton.
    3. Jean Frappier, *Chrétien de Troyes: The Man and His Work*, trans. Raymond J. Cormier (Athens: Ohio University Press, 1982), 4.

for a bourgeois approaching a woman of his own class, a woman of the nobility, and a woman of great nobility; for a great nobleman approaching a woman of his own rank, a woman of lesser nobility, and so forth. Peasant women may be taken by force. Clerics should not love, but since they are human beings and therefore imperfect they often will, so etiquette is prescribed for them too. Nuns, significantly, are denied any possibility of receiving carnal love.[4]

Another detail that might shed light on Chrétien's status is the fact that the rich and increasingly civilized courts of Champagne, Flanders, Burgundy, and elsewhere attracted men who had acquired humanistic learning, or *clergie*, through the Church, and then took only minor orders or did not enter religious service at all. As Frappier points out,

> More men of letters than men of the church, such clerics in a way were also humanists. Ideally, they saw themselves responsible for the heritage and transmission of Latin and even Greek poetry. Ever mindful of the advice in the *Liber Sapientiae* [Book of Wisdom attributed to Solomon in the Middle Ages] they sought to cultivate and never conceal man's divine gifts—knowledge and wisdom. Thus a scriptural text justified their lofty desire and linked them to traditions of antiquity.[5]

These men contributed much to the life and activity of the courts, and no doubt many poets were produced from their ranks. As for Chrétien, the prologue to *Erec and Enide* expresses just such a humanistic view as that described by Frappier: humans have an obligation to study, learn, and teach what is right, so that precious

4. Andreas Capellanus, *The Art of Courtly Love*, trans. John Jay Perry, ed. Frederick W. Locke (New York: Frederick Ungar, 1957), 5–24.

5. *Chrétien*, 10.

knowledge will not be lost. Witty and offhand as Chrétien's narrative voice frequently is, one senses in this opening passage the urgency of his convictions. At the end of the poem another passage demonstrates the importance of *clergie,* of the divine gift of knowledge for those powerful on earth: Erec's coronation robe bears the allegorical images of the four disciplines of the quadrivium, woven by magic. A great king must rule with the assistance of these disciplines, for it is through them that we comprehend our universe. Given such passages (and others showing reverence for Ovid and Virgil) it seems probable that Chrétien was a cleric of some sort, trained, perhaps, in the thriving schools at Troyes.

Troyes in Chrétien's period was a cosmopolitan center; it was one of the great fair towns of Europe (of which several existed in Champagne). These fairs occurred twice yearly in Troyes, and traders and entertainers gathered there from most corners of the known world. In Henri Pirenne's words, "the commercial expansion . . . spread like a beneficent epidemic over the whole Continent," and the famous fairs "fulfilled . . . the functions of an exchange and clearing house."[6] Chrétien's verse is full of descriptions—props for the rich fantasy of his courtly audience—of splendid goods from distant lands: opulent fabrics, such as "the silk called *escarlate,"* or "the silk called *osterin,"* or sendal (another silk, resembling taffeta); rubies, emeralds, and other gems; a saddle with ivory trimmings on which is carved the story of Aeneas; cloves, cinnamon, and other spices; exotic dyes in brilliant colors. After the First Crusade and on into the twelfth century, as trade expanded and the provincial courts grew richer, such luxuries as Chrétien describes were much in vogue. The great fairs were clearinghouses for art and ideas as well.

6. *Medieval Cities: Their Origins and the Revival of Trade,* trans. Frank D. Halsey (Princeton: Princeton University Press, 1925), 74.

No doubt a Norman or a Londoner—for that matter a Russian or an Icelander—could hear Provençal troubadour songs on the streets of Troyes, or the northern French trouvère songs of Chrétien's generation. One might hear Arab music and poetry or a Breton *conteur* reciting a Celtic legend of King Arthur or King Bran, imported over the centuries from Wales and Ireland.

In this city, for at least part of Chrétien's lifetime, the court of Champagne assembled. Countess Marie, like her mother, Eleanor of Aquitaine (and her sister, Aélis of Blois), promulgated the code of *courtoisie,* or refined and aristocratic manners, which included courtly love. The nature, extent, and influence of courtly love are vexed questions in the scholarship of our own time.[7] We can safely say that in addition to the masculine and military ethic of chivalry— embracing valor, piety, loyalty, honor, and so forth—courtly love entailed values of refinement and sensitivity, as Frappier remarks,

The highest qualities of the epic hero were preserved in the courtly hero: he had prowess (from *preux,* "brave") and was *courtois,* two characteristics often associated in the twelfth- and thirteenth-century romances. All this implied pride of lineage and control of self. But to these must henceforth be added other qualities, suitable to a more sophisticated social life, for example, refinement of language, manners, and clothing, a scrupulous loyalty in battle, *largesse* ("liberality," "generosity"), physical beauty, and, similarly, strength and courage. Perfect courtliness also involved respect for the actions and feelings of others, however disconcerting; this in turn inspired a predilection for moral nuances on the part of those rare individuals, the elite who

7. For a most thorough, sage, and illuminating review of studies of this subject, see Roger Boase, *The Origin and Meaning of Courtly Love: A Critical Study of European Scholarship* (Manchester: Manchester University Press, 1977).

evaluated themselves above the common order by dint of their inbred nobility or through their generous but hidden thoughts.[8]

For *fin' amors*—*courtoisie* in its more precise and limited sense—we have the evidence of the troubadours and trouvères; we have the definition and codification of love given by Andreas Capellanus (however seriously it was taken by his audience); and we have the poetry of the early romance writers. Chrétien's ideas on the subject seem to have differed from those in fashion at Marie's court. The prologue to his *Lancelot* strongly suggests that he wrote this work, a story of adulterous love between the hero and Queen Guinevere, at the behest of his patroness, not that of his muse. He appears to have resisted the notion of love as something intensely secret, painful, exalted, and adulterous, unrelated to the primarily economic and dynastic institution of marriage.

Indeed he appears to assert that marriage and love are the proper culmination of each other. In *Erec* and *Yvain,* the two romances with the most unified structure, the hero's problem is how to bring the demands of a man's external life—honor, reputation, hardihood, skill, noble acts toward others—into balance with the internal exploration, the growth and refinement of the spirit, made possible by erotic, conjugal love. Both the internal and the external virtues are absolutely necessary for the development of the chevalier. Courtly chivalry, at least as Chrétien conceived it, implies continuous effort, progress, *perfectionnement;* a static existence is a spiritual and moral death for the knight, as we shall see in the resolution of the *Erec.* The knight seeks a quest, or *avanture;* the word *avanture* is related to the word *avant*—that which lies *before* him, which he must accomplish to realize his implicit powers. The demands of action

8. *Chrétien,* 7.

and service (specifically service in love) are great and are constantly changing. To be a true chevalier, a full man and a noble one, the hero must have the fullness and readiness of spirit for both these demands.

Such, then, were the formative influences on Chrétien: chivalry, *courtoisie, clergie,* and the richness and variety of the civilization of his time. He is a civilized writer; Erich Auerbach, in his celebrated study *Mimesis,* speaks of the "natural narrative style" and the "impression of . . . fresh and easy breadth" in Chrétien's poetic voice, while remarking on the subtlety of structure in *Yvain* and the "analytical skill" evident in Chrétien's use of rhetorical devices.[9] To structure the poem as a whole, Chrétien uses *entrelacement*—the interlacing of subplots, a convention of the long medieval narrative —and *annulation,* a circular movement of plot whereby a threatening situation resembles one encountered earlier in the story but is more difficult, thus requiring more courage and maturity of the protagonist. Woven into these structures is what might be called a "language of portents," which sometimes seems to suggest a formal symbolic system and at other times seems to play, shrewdly and ironically, with the expectations a symbolic system sets up. There is much compelling allegory, some obvious, some less apparent to a modern sensibility; but nearly always the personifications are so supple and skillfully wrought that the allegory does not offend a modern reader. Chrétien has an extraordinary ability to combine eerie, fantastic subjects with worldly, shrewd attitudes; he gives a Celtic tale of the supernatural a down-to-earth setting and interpretation, without losing for his audience the dimension of the

9. *Mimesis: The Representation of Reality in Western Literature,* trans. Willard R. Trask (Princeton: Princeton University Press, 1953), 128.

mysterious. One sometimes suspects him of mischief, as when he claims that a castle, bestowed by Erec on his impoverished father-in-law, was built in the time of Adam; or when, with arcane slyness, he slips ludicrous characters into the procession of guests at Erec and Enide's wedding (see n. 13).

Chrétien is a gifted poet in a demanding verse form. Although the octosyllabic rhymed couplet puts strict limitations on its user, when properly handled it is a form of great suppleness, adaptability, and grace. In Chrétien's time Old French verse was accentual-syllabic, and thus not unlike modern English in meter and rhythm. In long narratives such verse establishes a cumulative, complex, and subtle movement. Often a skillful poet, like Chrétien or Chaucer, can establish a counterpoint between the syntactical movement of a sentence and the structure of the verse by judiciously using enjambment, choosing sound values that make rhymes emphatic or unemphatic, or quickening or slowing the pace of the narrative.

Chrétien repeats certain rhymes or certain lines for thematic emphasis; one particularly compelling example is "Cil dormi et cele veilla" (Roques ed., 2475, 3093; paraphrased at 3446–47): "He was asleep, and she awake." Here the young wife watches over her husband while he lies in great moral, or mortal, danger, in the shifting episodes of their adventurous life. The repetition of this line helps us see how their relationship changes, since in the second instance (and the paraphrase) they are on strained terms and share no physical intimacy. Chrétien frequently uses rhyme to link a name with a personal quality, or he repeats a rhyme in two or three successive couplets for emphasis, or sometimes, it seems, for the sheer pleasure of his "fine careless rapture." In Chrétien *rime riche*—a fashion much employed in medieval French verse (and later in medieval English verse, including Chaucer)—often forms a pun, as in *genz* (people, folk) and *genz* (noble, handsome), or *foiz* (times, in the sense of number) and *foiz* (faith or promise). Sometimes the *rime riche* is not so much a pun as the same word used in different contexts, offering contrast ("Nature was able to / . . . she was not able to") or more subtle comparisons. Chrétien shows us that words have facets, like well-cut gems; he holds them up to the light for us and demonstrates how they reflect meaning in their surroundings, shifting them back and forth slightly in the *rime riche* couplets.

Onomatopoeia occurs here and there in Chrétien's verse, to great effect. One passage delightfully describes a stag hunt, with its hue and cry, its horns, and its baying dogs:

Li un cornent, li autre huient;
li chien apres le cerf s'esbruient,
corent, angressent et abaient;
li archier espessement traient.
(Roques ed., 119–22)

Horns exulted, people cried out,
dogs bayed and snapped and leaped about,
hurled themselves, savaging the deer,
tormenting him; the archers there
shot thick, quick volleys. . . .
(below, 123–27)

Many battle scenes in Chrétien are full of the hiss and crackle and crashing noises of combat, suggesting the rushing of horses and the clang of steel on steel or the crack of weapons on wooden and leather shields—the intense hostility as enemy knights confront each other. Unfortunately, no translation can reproduce the felicity of the opening couplet of the story: "Au jor du Pasque, au tans novel, / a Quaradigan, son chastel . . ." The *novel / chastel* rhyme is like the chime of a bell, ringing in the story with all its human and mortal complexities, against the backdrop of the fresh, hopeful, and renewing time of Easter.

THE STORY

In the poem's brief prologue, Chrétien quotes a proverb and makes a boast. We are told, first of all, that we may have overlooked something of great value, that the story we are about to hear has been all but ruined by hack storytellers (who make an ill-gotten living telling bits and pieces of the popular Celtic Arthurian tales). Chrétien then claims that he will resurrect this poor, fractured tale; with his *molt bele conjointure* he will give it form and beauty, and it will last forever.[10] The story itself has a tripartite structure. In the first part Erec, a young man not quite twenty-five, who has a brilliant reputation for valor but appears to have side-stepped the experience of love, suddenly (and rather impulsively) finds himself an excellent bride. In the second part, Erec's love for his young wife, Enide, appears to have taken the place of his valor as an all-consuming occupation, and with his reputation endangered, he and his wife set out on a series of difficult and hazardous adventures. In the third section, with the dilemma resolved, Erec faces a still more dangerous *avanture;* his mastery of it enables him and Enide to set free a couple even more trammeled by the conflicts and drives of their existence than they themselves had been. In the end Erec and Enide have "proved most royal," and we see King Arthur crown them the rulers of Erec's hereditary domain.

---

10. Such uses of the proverb and the boast were common in Chrétien's time. The proverb is frequently found at the beginning of a fabliau; the poet's boast of superiority is a convention of French epic.

As the story opens, Arthur's court is celebrating Easter. Arthurian romances frequently begin with a religious festival, whether Easter, Pentecost, or Christmas, against which we see the all too human actions of the characters, with their weaknesses and their idealistic striving for *perfectionnement*. The beautiful Middle English *Sir Gawain and the Green Knight* likewise begins and ends with celebrations of Christmas and New Year, and we see the round of the year, the demarcation of human time and limitation and striving, against the implicit and explicit religious background of the work

In *Erec and Enide*, King Arthur has rather willfully revived an ancient custom, a courtly entertainment; it is one that virtually demands that each participant have a lady to love and serve, as of course every chevalier should. A hunt for a white stag is planned, and the captor must kiss the loveliest lady at court (presumably his own!). The hero, Erec, has no *amie*, or lady love, and so he lags behind, all but avoiding this courtly exercise. Setting off by himself, he encounters Queen Guinevere and offers to accompany her to the hunt, but they lose their way in the woods and come upon a vicious little band of strangers—a knight, his haughty *amie*, and a dwarf with a whip—who insult the queen and her party. Erec sets off after this knight to avenge the insult.

Already we see the language of portents, which would have been immediately recognized by Chrétien's audience, at work in the story. In the Celtic tales Chrétien and Marie de France employ, white stags, and white animals generally, are often guides to the Other World; sometimes they lead the hero to a supernatural encounter, for example with a supernally beautiful fairy mistress.[11]

11. Süheylâ Bayrav, *Symbolisme médiéval: Béroul, Marie, Chrétien* (Paris: Presses Universitaires de France, 1957), 204. For a compelling example from Marie de France, with a very interesting correlation to *Erec,* see Marie's *lai Guigemar.* There

Dwarfs are frequently portents of the supernatural and of evil.[12] In this instance, however, after we, *la crème* of Champagne, have been led to expect such an encounter, we see the hero enter a very real medieval town, where people are sweeping rooms, currying horses, and sitting about playing chess and throwing dice. Here Erec encounters an impoverished vavasor (a "vassal's vassal," or minor nobleman) and his lovely daughter, a young girl who performs the humblest tasks of house and stable and who wears a dress (white, significantly) so shabby that her elbows poke through the holes in her sleeves. Erec has avoided the stag hunt; now he involves himself in a ritual with far more serious consequences. He engages to champion the vavasor's daughter in a joust with the knight he is

---

the young hero goes to hunt a stag but instead finds a doe, all white and bearing antlers, with her fawn. He shoots her and she falls, but the arrow bounces back, wounding Guigemar through the right thigh and also wounding his horse. The dying deer speaks, saying that nothing will heal Guigemar's wound but a woman who will love him and suffer untold pain and grief for her love (81–122). The sexual imagery in this beautiful tale of developing adolescence is clear enough. Guigemar, like Erec, is a young man who has avoided the complications of love; he is full of "aggressive self-sufficiency and repressive chastity," as Robert Hanning and Joan Ferrante remark in an excellent discussion in their *Lais of Marie de France* (New York: E. P. Dutton, 1978), 55–59. In his attempt to deny the erotic side of his nature, or to obliterate the erotic urge as he knows it, the young huntsman succeeds only in nearly castrating himself, before a woman appears who delivers him from his plight.

12. A sinister dwarf drives the cart, a sort of tumbril for criminals, in Chrétien's *Lancelot*. See also Béroul's *Romance of Tristan,* trans. Alan S. Frederick (Harmondsworth: Penguin Books, 1970). The translator has an illuminating discussion of the tradition of evil dwarfs in medieval literature (see 16–17). But dwarfs could be portentous in other ways; see my discussion of Guivret le Petit and of Oberon in *Huon de Bordeaux,* below.

pursuing; he also proposes to marry the girl and take her to his own domain. The prize of the joust is a sparrow hawk, to be bestowed on the winner's lady. Erec wins this joust and sends the knight packing to Arthur's court; then he reiterates his serious intention of marrying the girl.

After much celebration with her family, he returns with the girl to court. She still wears her shabby white dress, which symbolizes her purity but also suggests a connection with the white stag (which did, indirectly, bring the couple together and guide Erec to his destiny). One might wonder whether there is something uncanny about this mysterious bride, so modest and beautiful yet so strangely dressed, whom Erec has won so precipitately. How will she assist in his development? Might she present some hidden danger to him? Thus Chrétien plays with our expectations. The couple is received with great honor at Arthur's court, where all concede that Enide is the loveliest woman present. Arthur, who killed the white stag, confers the ceremonial kiss upon her. Thus ends the first section of the story, which Chrétien refers to as the *premier vers* and which serves as a kind of overture in which the major themes are introduced.

There is a lavish wedding, with a guest list that evokes many tales from Celtic legend, as well as other figures of more recherché medieval lore. [13] A splendid tourney follows, and then the young couple departs for Erec's ancestral home of Estre-Gales (Outer Wales, or

13. Ferdinand Lot, "Les Noces d'Érec et d'Enide," *Romania* 66 (1920): 42–45, notes that in the *Etymologies* of Isidore of Seville, the Antipodes (in Libya) are reported to have feet pointing backward, with eight toes to each foot, and suggests that Chrétien, with Isidore's report in mind, was having fun with the wedding guest list.

southern Wales). Here they take up their roles as heir and heiress apparent. But Erec has shifted to a completely different mode of life; the brilliant chevalier has become uxorious, all but abandoning the outward questing life of the knight for the comforts and explorations of love. The lady is no supernatural lover, like those in Celtic stories; but with a power all too devastating in the natural world, she has inspired a love that threatens to destroy his knightly prowess and his will. She learns of his loss of reputation and is grief-stricken; he then learns of it through her.

His shame and anger (anger primarily at himself, though he only partly realizes it) are insupportable to him. He orders Enide to accompany him on another quest. She is to ride in front of him, in her most magnificent dress, and is not to speak to him unless he addresses her. In the Welsh tale *Geraint Son of Erbin,* thought to be an analogue, the young wife is made to wear her shabby dress in order to humiliate her; this detail has thematic symmetry. But in Chrétien's poem the wife rides in ironic magnificence, displaying the wealth her princely husband bestowed upon her—quite a contrast, this scene, from that in which the beloved betrothed is proudly presented to court in her rags and astonishing loveliness. In both stories the couple travels in silence, unattended, declaring no destination to anyone. Riding in front, Enide is obviously a lure, greatly increasing their danger and the difficulty of the test Erec has set himself.

Danger presents itself soon enough. First a band of three robbers appears and is defeated by Erec; very soon afterward a second group, of five this time, attacks, and Erec overcomes them as well, but in a more prolonged and bloodier fight. There is a structural logic in the way the second episode follows the first; this *annulation* emphasizes the cyclical, repetitive character of the story and prepares us for further paired incidents.

The other pairs do not occur in tandem but are interlaced. Two vicious, lustful counts—one pathologically vain (we would say he had a Don Juan complex), the other brutish—attempt to possess Enide. The first visits the couple, tries to seduce the wife, and plots to murder the wounded husband; the second, carrying the couple by force to his castle, believes Erec dead and, there under his own roof, forces Enide to marry him. As allegorical figures these two noblemen obviously represent aspects of lust. Both men are stupid; both present real danger. They suggest, allegorically, a mindless willfulness and violence in the sex drive. A third pair of incidents concerns Guivret le Petit, the proud, valiant, and generous dwarf-king, who must challenge and vanquish all knights who approach his domain. He battles with Erec and loses, only to become his deeply devoted companion; later he fights Erec nearly to the death without recognizing him (in armor, at night), then has him nursed back to health and vigor. Guivret may represent pride in its subtler, more engaging forms, pride as it occurs so often in nature, blended with the greatest of human virtues and thus very likely to deceive us. He may, somewhat like Una's dwarf in Spenser's *Faerie Queene* (who probably represents human reason), stand for confused and well-meaning (if proud and sometimes blind) human perception in general. Or like the good and valorous dwarf-king Oberon in *Huon de Bordeaux,* a French romance written about 1220, he may be a reminder to us that gallantry and generosity can come in strange forms.

Other incidents are paired, or refer to each other, in less obvious ways. At one point Erec, still suffering the acute shame and self-rejection of his *recreantise,* or lassitude, tries to avoid meeting with Arthur's court but is skillfully drawn there by Gawain; there his severe wounds are attended to. At the end of the romance a victorious Erec unexpectedly visits a sick and depressed Arthur; this time

Erec restores his liege to joy and well-being. Elsewhere the knight Yder, with whom Erec jousted to win the prize hawk for Enide, prefigures the knight Maboagrain in the Joy of the Court.

This episode, in the last section of the romance, tells of how Erec frees Maboagrain from the spell by which his *amie* has held him prisoner for years. The incident has intriguing Celtic trappings: the lush, burgeoning orchard-prison with its invisible wall of air, reminiscent of legends of the Celtic Other World; the motif of the Rash Promise, in which one person (a lover or a heroic figure) promises another unconditionally to grant any wish he or she might express; and the possible similarity to the legend of Merlin, whose *amie* tricked him and imprisoned him forever. In Chrétien's *conjointure* the Joy of the Court demonstrates Erec's ability to liberate and restore others, having achieved mastery over himself. Maboagrain and his lady, in their initial selfishness, compulsiveness, and limitation, are contrasted with the hero and heroine, who have grown beyond stasis and a wasteful expense of spirit.

Erec and Enide is unique among chivalric romances in that the woman, as well as the man, undergoes trials of worth and character. Enide is tested in virtues that are traditionally masculine—valor, loyalty, courtesy, readiness, perception of another person's plight —yet the psychological challenges that confront her, and her wise resolution of them, are what Chrétien's original audience would have considered properly feminine. Faced initially with a very difficult dilemma—whether to tell her husband of his *recreantise* and risk offending him, or let him continue in a lassitude that chivalry and morality forbid—she is at length forced to make the latter, more courageous, choice. She does not have the self-knowledge to take satisfaction in her courage but continually berates herself for false pride and ingratitude to her husband. At first she fears Erec will simply exile her; when, on their journey, she must act as a lure to danger and is forbidden to warn Erec, she follows her own good judgment (while undergoing an extremely painful psychological struggle), even if that means disobeying him (no easy decision for a woman of that period and culture). Tempted by another man while her own husband treats her with scorn, she remains chaste; threatened or coerced by other men, she defies or outwits them. She is constantly alert to Erec's needs and serves him as nurse, horse driver, and sentinel. In the Joy of the Court episode, their own differences having been resolved, only Enide can restore the self-willed, obsessive lady of the orchard to a state of health and generosity, of genuine love without fear or sterile possessiveness. Portrayed at the beginning of the story as a gentle, quietly competent girl, she appears at the end to be a portrait of chivalry in the female; not, most certainly, an Amazon, but the embodiment of knightly virtues in their female aspect, and the ideal of a chevalier's wife or a sovereign's consort.[14]

THE SCHOLARSHIP

A wide range of critical and scholarly methods have been employed in the examination of Chrétien's romances. In the early decades of this century his work was often explained as a mélange of adaptations of Celtic myth, at several removes from an imagined natural, or original, literary truth. Later scholarship, up until the 1970s,

---

14. Enide is sometimes compared to the long-suffering Griselda in Chaucer's *Clerk's Tale*. But because Enide rides into the wilderness on a quest, her trials resemble those of chivalry in a way that Griselda's do not; they complement her husband's trials. Moreover, Enide, though modest and deferential, has a tough, commonsense streak that seems lacking in Griselda.

tended toward historical studies or source studies.[15] The approaches of the past two decades have, in the main, been folkloric, anthropological and structural, rhetorical, sociohistorical, feminist, psychoanalytic, and deconstructionist.

The importance of Celtic legend, classical literature, and medieval symbolism has been exaggerated in interpretations of Chrétien's romances. Certain critics have found difficulties in motivation; why, for instance, does Erec treat Enide so harshly on their journey? His behavior, so inconsistent with the chivalric code, seems insufficiently explained. Roger Sherman Loomis believed that Erec's behavior might be based on Celtic sources, in which the model for Enide was Morgan la Fée, a lascivious enchantress over whom the hero must prevail. The idea is tantalizing, but Loomis does not provide sufficient evidence for it.[16] In *Geraint Son of Erbin,* the hero believes his wife to be in love with another man; while this explanation provides forceful motivation, the tale lacks the psychological subtlety of Chrétien's version of the story. Other interpretations suggest that Enide must, in the course of the tale, lose her exalted status as *amie* (in the courtly sense) and take on her role as obedient wife.[17] On the psychological level, it seems understandable

15. See the preface to Douglas Kelly's fine work, *Chrétien de Troyes: An Analytic Bibliography* (London: Grant and Cutler, 1976), where he remarks: "Chrétien scholarship is marked by a dichotomy between content and form, that is between emphasis on history and emphasis on archetype. . . . Specialization has narrowed: Celtic or Latin sources? Courtly love or Christian morality? Psychology or typology? Literary sociology or structuralism?" (11–12).

16. *Arthurian Tradition and Chrétien de Troyes* (New York: Columbia University Press, 1949), 120–27.

17. William A. Nitze, "The Romance of Erec, Son of Lac," *Modern Philology* 11 (1914): 445–89; esp. 447–50.

that Erec, an impulsive, quick-tempered, proud young man who has quite nearly lost his reputation, should in his wounded pride lash out at the one closest to him, she who seems to be the cause of his *recreantise*. That she appears to believe the gossip about Erec's failure of worth, and that she reproaches him and tells him what he must do, is even more galling to him. His actions are appropriate in a chivalric romance precisely because he must pass through this stage of immaturity in order to become, truly, a chevalier and a great prince. His obvious uncourtliness may also be a parody of courtly behavior or an ironic reflection of it.

Claude Luttrell, in his folkloric study, opposes many aspects of Loomis's claim that Chrétien was dependent on Celtic myth and traditional tale. Luttrell demonstrates Chrétien's originality through the poet's borrowings and rearrangements of material from the Fair Unknown type of folktale and through his use of ancient clerkly themes — such themes as the role of the goddess Nature in human affairs; the concept of human beauty as a mirror in which one can perceive one's ideal self (see *Erec*, 415–45, where we first see Enide through the narrator's eyes and the hero's); and the allegorization of figures such as Geometry and Astronomy (*Erec*, 6703–6760, from the description of the coronation).[18]

Medievalists have increasingly focused on a rhetorical issue: what Eugene Vance (discussing the work of Paul Zumthor) calls "the radical primacy of writing, whether as a pragmatic process or as an

18. *The Creation of the First Arthurian Romance* (Evanston, Ill.: Northwestern University Press, 1974). For a discussion of Nature, see 1–13; of portraiture, 14–25; of elements from clerical and classical learning, particularly Martianus Capella and Alain de Lille, 16–65; of elements of the international folktale type the Fair Unknown and Chrétien's innovative use of its motifs, 80–126 and passim.

ideological program, to modes of vernacular thought and expression."[19] Thus, in the chapter "Selfhood and Substance in *Erec et Enide*," Vance himself, meditating on the issue of whether "Erec's honor as a warrior [is] diminished by his ardor in love" and wondering whether Erec "can . . . be an ardent lover and remain a good warrior at the same time," concludes that "such questions involve more than the nature of heroic identity in romance; they implicate the very language and form of romance narrative itself. . . . Chrétien's task as a creator of narrative form," he adds, "is to 'invent' a coherent story where antimonies of language, mind and heroic action are fully expressed and 'conjoined,' rather than mutually suppressed."[20] Similarly, Donald Maddox foregrounds the medieval reader's experience of "the *written* textual document" to define *Erec et Enide* as "above all a problem-solving romance" in which a series of crucial "oppositions and tensions" (for instance, "chivalry vs. monarchy, higher vs. lower nobility, wealth vs. poverty, agnatic vs. matrilineal kinship identities") are "incrementally resolved through the dynamic discovery procedure of narrative."[21] Maddox brings to this rhetorical discussion a most astute anthropological and structural approach.

Addressing a more specific aspect of the problem of "textuality and authority" in medieval writings, Roberta L. Krueger has investigated the status of the narrative voice—the *je*—in Chrétien's romances and in the works of his successors. Krueger notes that "the question of the author—who is speaking, and in what voice?—re-

19. *From Topic to Tale: Logic and Narrativity in the Middle Ages* (Minneapolis: University of Minnesota Press, 1987), xxv; the preface contains a useful survey of the changing trends in the field of medieval studies from 1830 through the 1980s.

20. Ibid., 30.

21. *Structure and Sacring: The Systematic Kingdom in Chrétien's "Erec et Enide"* (Lexington, Ky.: French Forum Publishers, 1978), 16, 177, 178.

mains one of the fundamental problems which critics must confront in reading medieval romance. Inscribed in texts which embody the transformation from a traditional, oral culture to a self-reflective, written one, the narrative voice in medieval verse and prose romance is both fragmentary and multivalent."[22] Her central argument, moreover—that Chrétien's narrative voice is marked by "masterly ambiguity"—reinforces the claims for the centrality of textuality, or *writtenness,* made by critics from Zumthor to Maddox and Vance.

Other critics similarly focus on the rhetoricity of Chrétien's romances and those of his contemporaries. Peter Haidu shows how Chrétien used the rhetorical techniques of scholasticism, which were inherited from classical antiquity, depending on them greatly in his early romances but always adapting them to his own purposes, and in his later works achieving an aesthetic distance that is both ironic and moral. Thus Chrétien's "unique imagination" bespeaks the "delicate balance within the individual between the contradictory demands of his own nature and society."[23]

Douglas Kelly, in another rhetorical study, explores the imagination itself—not the common postromantic concept of utterly unbound, even "capricious" thought and artistic creation, but *Ymagination* as medieval people knew it. "Imagination," as Kelly points out, "is a mental faculty. It governs the invention, retention, and expression of Images in the mind; it also designates the artist's Image, projected as it were into matter." In this sense imagination is "a fundamental feature of the concept of art prevalent from the

22. Roberta L. Krueger, "The Author's Voice: Narrators, Audiences, and the Problem of Interpretation," in *The Legacy of Chrétien de Troyes,* ed. Norris J. Lacy, Douglas Kelly, and Keith Busby (Amsterdam: Editions Rodolphi, 1987), 1: 114–40; see esp. 117.

23. Peter Haidu, *Aesthetic Distance in Chrétien de Troyes* (Geneva: Droz, 1968), 261–62, quote on 263.

twelfth to the fifteenth century," and its aesthetic exists in Chartrian thought and literature, classical and medieval rhetoric, medieval poetry (including troubadour lyric), and in the thought of Andreas Capellanus. Allegory depends on it, as do the intense psychological struggles (*psychomachia*), often allegorical, that occur in Chrétien.[24]

Of concern to feminists, a debate as to whether the interests of aristocratic women were promoted or frustrated by courtly literature has been ongoing since the early 1960s. On one side Reto Bezzola, Myrrha Lot-Borodine, and many others since have argued that women gained status, as audience and as literary subjects, in the chivalric romances; on the other side John Benton and, more recently, Georges Duby have asserted that the power and influence of aristocratic women were on the wane, as that of chivalric and clerical institutions grew. Their side of the debate has been supported, in Chrétien studies, by Marie-Noëlle Lefay-Toury, who sees women's status subverted in all of Chrétien's works. Roberta L. Krueger, in a recent article, speaks of the "profound ambivalence about women's position in court life" (particularly in *Yvain*). "The hypothesis of the female reader," she writes, "focuses our attention on the problem of gender in romance and reveals sexual tensions which qualify the ideology of chivalry."[25]

24. Douglas Kelly, *Medieval Imagination* (Madison: University of Wisconsin Press, 1978), xi–xii, 29, 45.

25. Reto Bezzola, "La Transformation des mœurs et le rôle de la femme dans la classe féodale du XIe siècle," in *Les Origines et la formation de la littérature courtoise en Occident (500–1200)* (Paris: Champion, 1960), 2:461–84; Myrrha Lot-Borodine, *De l'amour profane à l'amour sacré: études de psychologie sentimentale au moyen-âge* (Paris: Nizet, 1961), 15–18; John Benton, "Clio and Venus: A Historical View of Medieval Love," in *The Meaning of Courtly Love,* ed. F. X. Newman (Albany: State University of New York Press, 1981), 34–37; Georges Duby, *Le Chevalier, la femme, et le prêtre: le mariage dans la France féodale* (Paris: Hachette, 1981);

Erich Köhler's sociohistorical study, *Ideal und Wirklichkeit in der höfischen Epik* (1956; translated into French as *L'Aventure chevaleresque*), contains an excellent discussion of the figure of Arthur and the form of the Arthurian romance. In Arthur's court, where every chivalric ideal is set forth, he himself is primus inter pares; it is his knights, his barons, who are powerful and heroic. Arthur is never a true sovereign; he is the symbol of an ideal feudal state, the guarantor of a perfect human order.[26] As such he represents the social ideals encouraged by the great feudal houses of Champagne, Blois, and Flanders vis-à-vis the strong Capetian monarchy. This social view does much to explain why, although the avatar of his court, Arthur is often curiously feeble, endangered by outside forces and in need of deliverance by his vassals. His greatest virtue is his *largesce,* or liberality, and his bestowing of *dons,* or gifts, upon his knights. This role is clear, in *Erec,* lines 1736–84, where Enide is first presented at court and Arthur, bestowing the kiss, describes his own kingly role as the protector and executor of the laws of his ancestors. At the couple's wedding Arthur is described as "pas chiche," not stingy; a long catalogue follows of the splendid and various gifts he gives out, in great abundance, to all the guests. As

---

Marie-Noëlle Lefay-Toury, "Roman breton et mythes courtois: L'évolution du personnage féminin dans les romans de Chrétien de Troyes," *Cahiers de civilisation médiévale* 15 (1972): 193–204 and 283–293; Roberta L. Krueger, "Love, Honor, and the Exchange of Women in *Yvain:* Some Remarks on the Female Reader," *Romance Notes* 25 (Spring 1985): 302–3. E. Jane Burns, in an unpublished manuscript entitled "Bodytalk: When Women Speak in Old French Literature," maintains that in *Erec and Enide* women succeed in telling different versions of events from the men's versions, and by these "unsettling stories" disrupt the intention of the courtly ideal—to "fetishize" the woman's body, to reify her and silence her independent voice.

26. Erich Köhler, *L'Aventure chevaleresque* (Paris: Gallimard, 1974), 26.

a prince Erec, too, displays *largesce;* he is compared to that legend of liberality, Alexander the Great (2213–14). Even in his blind uxoriousness, he regularly bestows rich gifts on his vassals, showing that traces of the great man remain (2446–51).

Köhler believes that in the twelfth century, when worldly and philosophical influences first created the concept of the individual in Western culture, a rupture occurred in the way people saw themselves; irrevocably, they were now individual as well as communal beings. In the Utopia of Arthur's court, Köhler sees a nostalgia for an older, more unified vision of human existence, and an attempt, albeit tentative and idealized, to reconcile the split in human consciousness through the integration of knightly heroes in the Arthurian court.[27] Like Donald Maddox, Köhler, from a somewhat different perspective, sees a dialectic in these works, a human struggle based on political and social forces.

Finally, the example of the Joy of the Court, an episode that has long puzzled interpreters, shows how new critical and theoretical strategies have enriched readings of Chrétien. The nineteenth-century scholar Gaston Paris called this last *aventure* a "récit absurde" and "incohérent";[28] Tennyson has been praised for excising it from his version of the story ("Geraint and Enid") in *The Idylls of the King.* Folklorists have devoted much speculation, on etymological and mythological grounds, to the significance of the words *Joy* and *Court.* Is Maboagrain, the captive knight, linked in ancient tradition with King Bran, with the Gallo-Roman Apollo Maponos and his supposed descendant Mabuz (from the Swiss *Lanzelet*), and with the Fisher King? Is the Joy then that of the Grail, and is *Court* a misreading of *cor* (horn) or *cors* (body, i.e., of Christ)? For Loomis

27. Ibid., 290–93.
28. Gaston Paris, *Romania* 20 (1891): 154.

these are important questions; for Luttrell they are pure skylark-ing.[29] However intriguing Loomis's conclusions may be (supported as they are with massive detail), modern scholars generally feel that he has not proved his case for the dominance of Celtic myth. For Charles Méla the episode lends itself to a resonant Lacanian analysis, in which a stable system of signification associated with the hier-archy of the court and the cultural identity that reputation, or *nom*, represents is disrupted by unknown or uncanny figures who quite literally embody the unknowability and insatiability of desire.[30] Roger Dragonetti notes that along with the powerful visual imagery of Arthurian material there is in Chrétien a *pur jeu phonique* (the term is Méla's, 32)—a euphonious, subtle, psychologically powerful pattern of diction that reinforces the numinous power of the poet's strange images and even the names of his characters.[31]

To be sure, this episode of the Joy of the Court has many narrative antecedents and analogues, ranging from the Celtic tales of the Other World inhabited by the Sidhe to the Kalypso episode in the *Odyssey*. Indeed, although Chrétien was most likely not alluding to Homer, the tale of Odysseus and Kalypso is curiously relevant here. For seven years the Greek wanderer lives imprisoned, compelled by the supernatural powers of the nymph Kalypso to remain and make love to her, though he is weary of her. The nymph has given him

---

29. Loomis, *Arthurian Tradition*, 168–84; Luttrell, *Creation*, 242.

30. See his brilliant discussion in *La Reine et le Graal: La conjointure dans les romans du Graal, de Chrétien de Troyes au livre de Lancelot* (Paris: Seuil, 1984), esp. chap. 1, 25–42.

31. Dragonetti, *La Vie de la lettre au moyen-âge* (Paris: Seuil, 1980); see esp. 32–34, where he speculates that Chrétien deliberately plays with aural overtones of classical material. Thus *Erec*, or the old form *Guerec*, suggests *Grec*; and *Enide* suggests *Enee*, or Aeneas—hence her beautiful saddle carved with figures from the *Aeneid*. Enide is thus, Dragonetti puns, truly "une chrétienne de Troie."

immortality; they live amid the beauty of lush, teeming natural surroundings; yet he is miserable and appears to be undergoing a spiritual death. In the Joy of the Court, Maboagrain remains captive in a lush orchard for seven years, bound to do the bidding of his *amie;* his is an existence with no future, no *avanture,* no engagement in the world and the community, but only plethora and dalliance, the glutted sterility of Luxuria. Like Odysseus and like Erec and Enide, Maboagrain must escape into the mortal world of change and uncertainty.

A NOTE ON THE TRANSLATION

There is a recent edition of *Erec and Enide,* in Old French with a literal, line-by-line English translation, by Carleton W. Carroll.[32] I have found this work very useful, but it was published when I was on the point of completing my own verse translation. The text on which this translation is based is the Guiot manuscript, or B.N. 794, probably the best text extant and certainly one of the earliest. In a very few instances, where the Guiot MS did not provide lines that seemed to clarify the sense of a passage, I have added lines, a couplet or two in nearly every instance, from a second manuscript, B.N. 1450. Sixteen lines missing from the Guiot MS at the very end of the poem I have also supplied from B.N. 1450, since they provide a better resolution. These additions, which amount to fewer than twenty-five lines in all, are signaled by brackets in the text and are indicated, with discussion where necessary, in the notes.

---

32. Chrétien de Troyes, *Erec and Enide,* ed. and trans. Carleton W. Carroll, with an introduction by W. W. Kibler (New York: Garland Publishing, 1987).

Chrétien's rhymed octosyllabic verse form has a wit, precision, and tautness unlike anything that can be reproduced in prose or in blank verse. Form is inevitably part of meaning; the effects of meter, rhythm, and rhyme are an essential part of Chrétien's narrative art. Poems written in strict forms are elegant cages of sound—sound that bounds around—and it is that echoing, reverberating structure that suggests, as nothing else does, the agility, the reflections, the cumulative power of Chrétien's story.

A verse translator works with a list of compelling priorities, one that demands constant reexamination. Meter must be absolutely right; rhythm must be appropriate, whether rapid, slow, smooth, or broken unexpectedly for a purpose. At times the rhythm may be like a glassy river with scarcely a ripple; at other times it will "work like a sea." Rhyme must be consistently effective, without too monotonous a chime. George Saintsbury remarked that octosyllabic verse in English has a "fatal fluency," which can create an effect of trivial patter; one must avoid that effect and yet achieve a constant smoothness and versatility.

Added to these considerations is of course the consideration of fidelity—or rather, fidelities. There is the narrative voice to consider, as well as the individual voices of characters and of situations. In an ironic, witty poet such as Chrétien, there are nuances of humor, understatement, and juxtaposition; there are all the nuances of psychological exploration. One must reach out to a mind and voice that existed eight hundred years ago, confident that one apprehends some of that consciousness but always wary of misinterpretation. Always there is the problem of diction. One can avoid fustian archaism, as I have done my best to do; one can avoid a jarring anachronistic slang; yet the problem of how to render Chrétien's voice in easy, graceful, appropriate twentieth-century

English remains. As I have remarked elsewhere,[33] all translators of past literature are Psyche: all of us must struggle to understand the shadowy prince we live with, and call on our best powers to interpret his spirit and give it force in our world. There are times when our labors of love can resemble Psyche's; they can seem to be the sorting of immense piles of seeds. But it is only by such labors that we can accomplish our task; otherwise, as Chrétien reminds us, much that is of value will be hidden or lost.

In general I have tried to follow Chrétien's prosodic practice as closely as possible. Where I could not reproduce a specific effect, such as *rime riche,* in a specific passage, I employed the effect later, without, I believe, sacrificing semantic accuracy. Here and there I permitted myself the sort of puns and plays on words that are part of Chrétien's style but that I was not always able to reproduce at the points where they occur in the original. In places I tried to work into the verse an explanation required by a modern reader, to save the reader the trouble of a footnote. Chrétien, like many medieval writers, changes verb tenses from preterite to present and back again in short passages, sometimes in midsentence. This practice, confusing and distracting to a contemporary reader, I have avoided, putting most of the story in the preterite and occasionally setting a scene in the present tense to create an effect of urgency and immediacy. For concepts central to the work or to the age in which Chrétien lived, I have retained the Old French vocabulary, believing it essentially untranslatable and hoping thereby to give the reader a view, however small and evanescent, into that vanished world. Such words as *avanture* and *recreant* I left untranslated. I made a point of including, in translation, such expressions as *biax sire* (fair sire) and

33. " 'But Why Are You Doing It in *Verse?*' Further Thoughts on Translating the Poet of Champagne," *Translation Review,* no. 27 (1988): 10.

biax dolce amie (fair, sweet friend), which convey the *politesse* that is so much part of the behavior of Chrétien's characters.

Peter Whigham once wrote of verse translation, "If the translator has failed to write a poem, he has done nothing. But if that's all he's done, he's not done enough. A poem that's a translation is required to be continually illuminating of its original."[34] That task, so simply and straightforwardly described but so infinitely complex in execution, is what I have attempted here. I hope that in doing so I have represented some of the virtues of this noble poet, whose mind and voice, while often obscure to Anglophone readers, have been so influential in our culture.

34. Peter Whigham, *Do's and Don'ts of Translation* (Isla Vista, Calif.: Turkey Press, 1982), 1.

Suggestions for Further Reading

EDITIONS

Chrétien de Troyes. *Erec and Enide.* Ed. and trans. Carleton W. Carroll, with an introduction by William W. Kibler. Garland Library of Medieval Literature, no. 25. New York: Garland Publishing, 1987. The edition is based on the Guiot MS (B.N. 794), with some emendations; the translation is literal and in free verse.

——. *Erec et Enide.* Vol. 1 of *Les Romans de Chrétien de Troyes.* Ed. Mario Roques. Les Classiques Français du Moyen Age, no. 80. Paris: Champion, 1952.

REFERENCE

Flutre, Louis-Fernand. *Table des noms propres avec toutes leurs variantes figurant dans les romans du moyen-âge écrits en français ou en provençal.* Poitiers: Centre d'études supérieures de civilisation médiévale, 1962.

Kibler, William H. *An Introduction to Old French.* New York: Modern Language Association of America, 1984.

West, G. D. *French Arthurian Prose Romances: An Index of Proper Names.* Toronto: University of Toronto Press, 1978.

——. *French Arthurian Verse Romances, 1150–1300: An Index of Proper Names.* Toronto: University of Toronto Press, 1969.

MEDIEVAL WORKS

Alain de Lille, *Anticlaudianus: or The Good and Perfect Man.* Trans. James J. Sheridan. Toronto: Pontifical Institute of Medieval Studies, 1983.

——. *The Complaint of Nature.* Trans. Douglas M. Moffat. New York: Henry Holt, 1908.

Béroul. *The Romance of Tristan.* Trans. Alan S. Frederick. Harmondsworth: Penguin Books, 1970.

Capellanus, Andreas. *The Art of Courtly Love.* Trans. John Jay Perry. Ed. Frederick W. Locke. New York: Frederick Ungar, 1957.

Chrétien de Troyes. *Arthurian Romances.* Trans. William W. Kibler, except *Erec and Enide* trans. Carleton W. Carroll. New York: Penguin Books, 1991.

——. *Arthurian Romances.* Ed. and trans. D. D. R. Owen. New York: E. P. Dutton, 1987.

——. *Perceval, or the Story of the Grail.* Trans. Ruth Harwood Cline. Athens: University of Georgia Press, 1983. Rhymed verse translation.

——. *Yvain, or the Knight with the Lion.* Trans. Ruth Harwood Cline. Athens: University of Georgia Press, 1975. Rhymed verse translation.

The Mabinogion. Trans. Gwyn Jones and Thomas Jones. New York: E. P. Dutton, 1949; rev. ed. by Gwyn Jones and Mair Jones, 1974. The Welsh analogue to *Erec, Geraint Son of Erbin,* appears on 229–73.

Marie de France. *The Lais of Marie de France.* Ed. and trans. Robert Hanning and Joan Ferrante. New York: E. P. Dutton, 1978.

SCHOLARLY AND CRITICAL WORKS

Auerbach, Erich. *Mimesis: The Representation of Reality in Western Literature.* Trans. Willard R. Trask. Princeton: Princeton University Press, 1953. See especially chapter 6, "The Knight Sets Forth" (123–42).

Bayrav, Süheylâ. *Symbolisme médiéval: Béroul, Marie, Chrétien.* Paris: Presses universitaires de France, 1957.

Benton, John F. "Clio and Venus: A Historical View of Medieval Love." In *The Meaning of Courtly Love,* ed. F. X. Newman. Albany: State University of New York Press, 1981.

———. "The Court of Champagne as a Literary Center," *Speculum* 36 (1961): 551–91.

Bezzola, Reto R. *Le Sens de l'aventure et de l'amour.* Paris: La Jeune Parque, 1947.

———. "La Transformation des mœurs et le rôle de la femme dans la classe féodale du XIᵉ siècle." In *Les Origines et la formation de la littérature courtoise en Occident (500–1200).* Paris: Champion, 1960.

Blaisdell, Foster W., and Mariann E. Kalinke. *Erex Saga and Ivens Saga: The Old Norse Versions of Erec and Yvain.* Lincoln: University of Nebraska Press, 1977.

Boase, Roger. *The Origin and Meaning of Courtly Love: A Critical Study of European Scholarship.* Manchester: Manchester University Press, 1977.

Curtius, Ernst Robert. *European Literature and the Latin Middle Ages.* Trans. Willard R. Trask. Princeton: Princeton University Press, 1953.

Dragonetti, Roger. *Le Gai Savoir dans la rhétorique courtoise.* Paris: Seuil, 1982.

———. *La Vie de la lettre au moyen-âge.* Paris: Seuil, 1980.

Duby, Georges. *Le Chevalier, la femme, et le prêtre: le mariage dans la France féodale.* Paris: Hachette, 1981.

———. *The Chivalrous Society.* Trans. Cynthia Paston. London: Edward Arnold, 1977.

Frappier, Jean. *Chrétien de Troyes: The Man and His Work.* Trans. Raymond J. Cormier. Athens: Ohio University Press, 1982.

Gies, Frances. *The Knight in History*. New York: Harper and Row, 1984.

Haidu, Peter. *Aesthetic Distance in Chrétien de Troyes*. Geneva: Droz, 1978.

Holmes, Urban Ticknor, Jr. *Daily Living in the Twelfth Century: Based on the Observations of Alexander Neckham in London and Paris*. Madison: University of Wisconsin Press, 1952.

Keen, Maurice. *Chivalry*. New Haven: Yale University Press, 1984.

Kelly, Douglas. *Chrétien de Troyes: An Analytic Bibliography*. London: Grant and Cutler, 1976.

———. *Medieval Imagination*. Madison: University of Wisconsin Press, 1978.

Köhler, Erich. *L'Aventure chevaleresque*. Trans. Eliane Kaufholz. Paris: Gallimard, 1974. Originally published as *Ideal und Wirklichkeit in der höfischen Epik*. Tübingen: Max Niemeyer, 1956.

Krueger, Roberta L. "The Author's Voice: Narrators, Audiences, and the Problem of Interpretation." In *The Legacy of Chrétien de Troyes*, ed. Norris J. Lacy, Douglas Kelly, and Keith Busby, 1: 114–40. Amsterdam: Editions Rodolphi, 1987.

———. "Love, Honor, and the Exchange of Women in *Yvain*: Some Remarks on the Female Reader." *Romance Notes* 25 (Spring 1985): 302–17.

LaBarge, Margaret Wade. *Medieval Travellers*. New York: W. W. Norton, 1983.

Lacy, Norris J. *The Craft of Chrétien de Troyes*. Leiden: E. J. Brill, 1980.

Lefay-Toury, Marie-Noëlle. "Roman breton et mythes courtois: l'évolution du personnage féminin dans les romans de Chrétien de Troyes." *Cahiers de civilisation médiévale* 15 (1972).

Loomis, Roger Sherman. *Arthurian Tradition and Chrétien de Troyes*. New York: Columbia University Press, 1949.

———. *The Development of Arthurian Romance*. New York: W. W. Norton, 1963.

Lot, Ferdinand. "Les Noces d'Erec et d'Enide," *Romania* 66 (1920): 42–45.

Lot-Borodine, Myrrha. *De l'amour profane à l'amour sacré: études de psychologie sentimentale au moyen-âge.* Paris: Nizet, 1961.

Luttrell, Claude. *The Creation of the First Arthurian Romance.* Evanston, Ill.: Northwestern University Press, 1974.

Maddox, Donald. *Structure and Sacring: The Systematic Kingdom in Chrétien's "Erec et Enide."* Lexington, Ky.: French Forum Publishers, 1978.

Méla, Charles. *La Reine et le Graal: la conjointure dans les romans du Graal, de Chrétien de Troyes au livre de Lancelot.* Paris: Seuil, 1984.

Muscatine, Charles. *Chaucer and the French Tradition.* Berkeley: University of California Press, 1957.

Nitze, William A. "The Romance of Erec, Son of Lac." *Modern Philology* 11 (1914): 445–89.

Pirenne, Henri. *Medieval Cities: Their Origins and the Revival of Trade.* Trans. Frank D. Halsey. Princeton: Princeton University Press, 1925.

Topsfield, L. T. *Chrétien de Troyes: A Study of the Arthurian Romances.* Cambridge: Cambridge University Press, 1981.

Vance, Eugene. *From Topic to Tale: Logic and Narrativity in the Middle Ages.* Minneapolis: University of Minnesota Press, 1987.

Vinaver, Eugene. *Form and Meaning in Medieval Romance.* Leeds: Maney, 1968.

Whigham, Peter. *Do's and Don'ts of Translation.* Isla Vista, Calif.: Turkey Press, 1982.

Zumthor, Paul. *Essai de poétique médiévale.* Paris: Seuil, 1972.

———. *Langue, texte, énigme.* Paris: Seuil, 1975.

EREC *and* ENIDE

THE PEASANT IN his proverb says
that a scorned object often is
truly a prize and a windfall;
so if a man is wise at all,   4
he makes good use of what he knows.
If he's assiduous, he shows
he uses what he has: he works;
for he who's negligent, and shirks   8
such duty, overlooks some treasure,
often, that would have given pleasure.
This is why Chrétien de Troyës
urges what's right; and why he says   12
Think! Spare no effort! Learn fair speech,
Learn how to well and truly teach.
A tale of *avanture* he'll tell,
beautifully joined and crafted well,   16
and when he does, he'll make his suit
that one is not at all astute
to hide his genius that God made,
or his light, in a bushel's shade.   20
This story of Erec, son of Lac—
broken, spoiled, by every hack
who pieces out and mars a tale
for kings and counts—I'll make prevail.   24
It shall endure in memory
as long as Christianity;
this is your Chrétien's boast. He says:
his tale shall live! He promises.   28

EASTER HAD COME, that time of year
when we feel re-created here
below, and all seems new again.
Arthur held court at Cardigan;   32
never, since world and time began,
had such a splendid, dazzling one
been seen, with such fine chevaliers,
hardy, combative, proud, and fierce,   36
women and girls so elegant,
princesses rich and radiant.
Before the court disbanded there,
Arthur had all his knights prepare   40
to hunt the white stag and restore
a custom honored long before.
    Sir Gawain felt sincere alarm,
and said, "Sire, not a thing but harm,   44
grief, and ill will can come of this.
We all know what this custom is!
The man who kills the stag will be
obliged, by right and courtesy,   48
whatever the cost or the import,
to kiss the loveliest girl at court.
No matter who's insulted, he
must offer up this gallantry.   52
What a disaster will ensue!
Here are five hundred women, who
are of high birth and character,
kings' daughters, of great savoir faire.   56
And each one in your entourage
has her own knight; he'll take umbrage!
Bold and audacious, wild with love,
each chevalier will have to prove,   60
rightly or wrongly, that the best
lady is his, and the loveliest."

The king said, "Yes, I know. But still,
I disregard this talk. My will   64
is to proceed; the plans are made.
The king's word should not be gainsaid.
Tomorrow a great company
will get an early start, and we   68
will have a splendid hunt, I'm sure,
in the forest of *avanture*."
So all was set; and in the dawn
they gathered, and the hunt was on.   72
    Day was just breaking when the king
got up; quickly appareling
himself, he put on last the short
tunic he wore for woodland sport.   76
And now the chevaliers awoke;
the hunters dressed, efficient folk,
got arrows, bows, as was their wont,
and hurried to the woods to hunt.   80
    After all these Queen Guinevere
mounted her horse; attending her
was her young maidservant, and she
—a princess—rode a good palfrey.   84
After these two, upon a course
as fast as he could prick his horse,
came a young knight, Erec by name,
of the Round Table. Honor, fame   88
were given to him abundantly.
No knight was praised as much as he
at court, and he was handsomer
than most men you'll see anywhere—   92
beautiful, noble, skillful, bold!
And not yet twenty-five years old.
Never had any man his age
shown such adroitness and courage.   96

Of his great virtues, what to say?
His destrier he rode that day,
sported an ermine cloak, and rode,
galloping, tearing up the road   100
in front of him. The drapery
of his silk tunic, you could see,
was Constantinople cloth, all fine
flowers of arabesque design.   104
Stockings he had, superbly cut,
of silk; his spurs were gold; he sat
firm in his stirrups. Accoutrements
of knightly honor and defense   108
—except his sword—he had not brought.
    He rode by a sharp bend and caught
up with the queen, and said to her:
"Madame, if it is your pleasure,   112
may I come ride along with you?
Nothing, you know, I'd rather do
than spend this time in your company."
Guinevere thanked him graciously.   116
"That would delight me, as you know,
fair friend; yes, join us, do. We'll go
together." So the party went
through woodlands toward the big event.   120
    Those who had started on the chase
flushed the deer from its hiding place.
Horns exulted, people cried out,
dogs bayed and snapped and leaped about,   124
hurled themselves, savaging the deer,
tormenting him; the archers there
shot quick, thick volleys. In the lead
was Arthur on his Spanish steed.   128
    In the forest Queen Guinevere
rode on, ears strained, and tried to hear

the dogs, and still her company
was Erec in his finery   132
and her attendant maid, who was
so lovely and so courteous.
But they were lost; these riders were
far from the thicket where the deer   136
was taken; they heard not a sound
of horn, of hunter, or of hound.
They turned; still straining ears they went,
trying to hear sounds of the hunt,   140
high cries of dogs, men's shouts in chase,
so they turned toward an open place,
a clearing down a path, and then
they stopped a moment in this glen.   144
Just then there drew within their sight,
armed, on a charger, a strange knight
with shield on shoulder, hand on lance.
The queen saw him at a distance;   148
and at his side there could be seen
a girl of proud and high-bred mien;
in front of them, on a draft horse,
there came a dwarf. Along the course,   152
all down the road, he led this band;
a knotted thong was in his hand.
    Guinevere saw, as they drew near,
the handsome, adroit chevalier,   156
she more and more grew curious
about this knight and who he was.
She bade her maid go instantly,
speak to the knight, make inquiry.   160
"Demoiselle," so said Guinevere,
"Go and speak to that chevalier.
Tell him to come, and bring as well
his lovely, elegant *pucelle*."   164

The girl went at an amble, right
along the road toward the knight.
But now the dwarf came up to meet her;
whip in hand, he came to greet her: 168
"Demoiselle, stop!" cried out this runt.
Nasty, he was, and arrogant.
"What do you think you're looking for?
Get back, you wench! Not one step more!"   172
"Dwarf," said she, "let me pass by.
I wish to speak to that knight, and I
am sent to do so by the queen."
The dwarf stood in the way. Obscene,   176
foul-smelling, filthy, he stood his ground.
"You won't do that, girl, I'll be bound.
Be off, you baggage! You've no right
to speak to such a noble knight."   180
      The girl moved forward on her horse,
thinking to gain her way by force,
impatient and contemptuous
of the crude little creature's fuss.   184
Then the dwarf raised his whip; as she
rode on, he snapped it viciously,
wanting to hit her in the face.
She raised her arm to shield the place;   188
he was alert, and struck her hand.
She saw where he had hit her, and
that her palm was already dark
bluish, and bruised from the thong's mark.   192
It would not do to persevere,
apparently, with this creature.
She turned around. Pain and surprise
made the tears pour down from her eyes,   196
wetting her whole face. Now the queen

did not know what to do, the scene
appalled her so. "Erec!" she cried.
"Fair friend, I am so mortified!   200
My poor *pucelle*! The shame, the grief!
This boorish knight's beyond belief!
That dwarf! Abortion, travesty
of nature, hurt her! How dare he!   204
Go to this knight, fair friend, and say
that he, and his lady too, must pay
at once, the courtesy of speech!
Say I demand as much, from each!"   208
    Erec went off. Toward the knight,
kicking his spurs, he rode; the sight
made the dwarf rush up to engage
Erec; he shouted in his rage.   212
"Vassal!" he spat. "Back, disappear!
I don't know what you're doing here,
or what you think you mean to do.
Get back, if you know what's good for you."   216
    "Move off!" said Erec, "loathsome dwarf!
You are too rude, you quarrelsome oaf.
Off, stand aside!" "Oh, no you don't!"
"Oh, yes I will!" "Oh, no, you won't!"   220
He pushed the dwarf then, vigorously.
Matchless in nastiness, though, he
—the whipster artist—gave Erec
a thorough lashing on the neck,   224
thus lacerating neck and face
where the thongs fell, and every place
from scalp to collarbone, now showed
stripes that the lashes had bestowed.   228
    Erec could see he'd have small joy
delivering equal courtesy,

for now he saw the chevalier,
armed and enraged, and he felt fear   232
that he himself would be killed off
if he were to attack the dwarf.
Always in such an argument
weapons are very eloquent.   236
Foolhardy is not brave, and then,
he who gives up can fight again.
    "Dame," said Erec, "see how this runt
disgraces me! Ha, some brave stunt,   240
slashing my face! Oh, the chagrin!
I dared not scratch his filthy skin,
bare as I am, and weaponless;
the knight knew I had no redress.   244
I feared to joust with him; he was
so brutal and discourteous.
It was no joke. His firm intent
was a sweet meal of pride; he meant   248
to make an end of me. *Alors,*
my queen, I promise that this score
will be made even! Oh, he'll pay
for shaming me! My arms today,   252
alas, I left at Cardigan,
thinking I did not need them when
I came this morning on the hunt.
If I go get them now, I won't   256
by any fortune hope to catch
this man, who's fled with such dispatch.
Let me give chase without delay!
Whether nearby or far away,   260
I'll find some arms; I'll rent them or
someone will lend me from their store.
Once I've got what I need, that knight

will find me apt enough to fight, 264
and not the man to flinch or quail!
Depend upon it, without fail
there will be combat. One thing's sure,
either I will subdue this boor, 268
or he will me. Now, if I can,
in three days I'll have found this man,
and I'll be back at court, elated
with my success—or devastated. 272
And now, Madame, I'll leave you here,
and settle with this chevalier.
God keep you. I am on my way."
The queen replied in kind, to pray 276
five hundred times and to commend
to God the safety of her friend.
    Now parted from Queen Guinevere,
Erec pursued the chevalier; 280
she waited in the forest. Here
the king at last had seized the deer,
and now, upon its capturing,
the knights came quickly, clustering 284
behind the king, in for the kill.
The hunt was done; they had their will,
and with their prize they must return.
They brought the stag to Cardigan. 288
    After supper, when all the knights
were full of jests and merry flights
of wit that rang from wall to wall,
the king proclaimed among them all 292
that now the rite must be fulfilled
for which the white stag had been killed.
Now was the moment for the kiss.
What murmurs, what uneasiness 296

now filled the court! What vows, what oaths,
muttered or hissed, now filled the mouths
of knights who, full of rage, each swore
to prove, by lance or ashwood spear,   300
his love was loveliest of all!
So foul words flew from wall to wall.
    And now, of course, my lord Gawain—
who, you remember, had foreseen   304
this great set-to—did not rejoice.
"Sire," he exclaimed, "you hear this noise.
You hear them fulminate and hiss!
They speak of nothing but this kiss.   308
The thing cannot be done, they say,
without a quarrelsome melee."
The king responded sensibly:
"Fair nephew Gawain, counsel me.   312
Assist my honor and my rights;
I want no brawls among these knights."
    Quickly to conclave now there came
the better barons, of most fame.   316
The king Ydiers was first to be
called up to serve this company.
King Cadiolanz assisted there,
a wise and valiant chevalier;   320
there was Sir Gilflez and Sir Kay,
King Amauguins, who had his say;
and with them all an adequate
group of good knights for the debate.   324
    Speech and debate had started, when
the queen came in the hall again.
She told them of the episode:
how, in the forest as she rode,   328
she met the chevalier, all armed,

and the vindictive dwarf, who harmed
her maid—he cracked his hateful whip,
and gave her hand a vicious rip;   332
and how the dwarf, with equal grace,
then struck Sir Erec in the face;
how Erec chased the knight to win
his damaged honor back again;   336
and how, in three days, if he could,
he would return, his vow made good.
    "Sire," said the queen, "defer a bit.
Here is my thought; consider it.   340
And you, my lords, consider this:
Lay this whole matter of the kiss
aside, till Erec's back again."
All thought this a judicious plan;   344
Arthur himself gave his consent.

꠸

EREC NOW FOLLOWED, all intent,
the knight, who now had sped apace,
with the churl dwarf who'd whipped his face,   348
until he saw a castle, which
was strong, well situated, rich;
they shot, pell-mell, right through the gate.
    All within seemed to celebrate   352
the joys of knights and maids, for all
were marvelously beautiful.
Some stroked and tended, in their walk,
a molting falcon, sparrow hawk,   356
a tiercel or a goshawk, mewed,
or else still young, and tawny-hued.
And there were games of many sorts:

hazards for stakes, dice, other sports,   360
backgammon, chess, and play at tables.
And young boys stood in front of stables
currying horses like good grooms,
and women swept and tended rooms.   364
And all these people saw, afar,
the knight, who was familiar,
with him his dwarf and fair lady.
All came to meet him, three by three,   368
with salutation and with praise,
but troubled with no courtesies
to Erec, whom they did not know.
But Erec followed still, and so   372
throughout the city went in chase
till the knight found a lodging place.
Erec was full of glee and mirth;
he'd run his quarry to its earth.   376
     Loitering briefly, he saw where
a man half lay upon a stair,
a man quite old, a vavasor;
his body, though, was humble and poor,   380
still he was handsome, debonair,
courtly in aspect, with white hair.
He seemed to be alone; he sat
apparently quite lost in thought.   384
He seemed a brave and valiant sort,
and Erec now came through the court
and hailed this man immediately.
The man ran up most courteously   388
and spoke before it had occurred
to Erec to select a word.
     "Fair sire," he said, "be welcome here.
Stay, and accept our bed and cheer.   392

See, your hostel's prepared for you."
"Thank you," said Erec, "I will do
just that; for I did hope to find
such lodging, and you're very kind."   396
Erec dismounted, these words said,
and the old man himself now led
the horse; he took it by the reins;
For his guest's joy he took such pains.   400
    The vavasor now called his dame
and lovely daughter, and they came
out from a workroom, as he bid;
I've no idea what work they did.   404
But now the wife came hurrying out,
and the young girl, wrapped all about
in a chemise, full-skirted, that
was pleated, white, and delicate;   408
above, a *chainse,* an overdress,
and nothing more and nothing less.
So old, the *chainse,* one could perceive
an elbow poking through each sleeve,   412
a shabby, poor exterior;
the hidden body, though, was fair!
    Indeed this girl was beautiful;
for Nature, who designs us all,   416
had on this favorite project spent
her every effort and intent;
more than five hundred times she thought
and marveled that she'd had the wit   420
to make—just once—so exquisite
a being, but never copy it.
She labored; but her arduousness
could not remake such loveliness.   424
Forced to bear witness, then, was Nature

to the rare beauty of this creature.
You should know that Iseult the Fair
had not such brilliant, shining hair,   428
such lovely golden hair as she,
so full of light and lambency.
The lily, the fresh fleur-de-lis,
had not her forehead's clarity,   432
her face and forehead's rosy pallor,
or her cheeks' fresh and rosy color—
a marvel underneath the white—
that made her eyes seem full of light.   436
And she had lovely, brilliant eyes,
like the stars scattering the skies;
never had God made half so well
nose, mouth, and eyes so beautiful.   440
Of such great beauty, what to say?
This girl was made, most certainly,
to be regarded, gazed upon,
eagerly, in the way that one   444
might look, and think, in one's own glass.
    Out of the workroom came this lass,
and she saw there the chevalier,
all unfamiliar, strange to her,   448
and she hung back a bit, for she
felt in his presence modesty.
Embarrassed, she blushed. And he felt awe
and fear, on his side, when he saw   452
beauty so rare and delicate.
    The vavasor cut in, "My sweet,
take now the horse of this good knight
into the stable for the night,   456
give him a place among our mounts.
See he lacks nothing that he wants:

take off his gear, put it away,
see that he has his oats and hay,   460
comb him, curry him, care for him,
see he's content, well fed, and trim."
     The girl goes off now with the mount,
undoes the breast strap at his front,   464
take off his saddle, bridle, reins;
see, now, how well she entertains
the tired beast—puts his halter on,
curries him, combs him, rubs him down,   468
at the manger takes off his halter,
gives him his hay and oats and water,
fresh wholesome grain—and then returns.
And when she does, her father turns   472
and says, "Dear daughter, show this lord
what courtesy we can afford:
lead him and take his hand in yours,
and show him now at once indoors;   476
his honor, you can see, is great."
And the girl did not hesitate,
for she was neither slow nor coarse.
She took his hand; they went indoors.   480
     The wife had slipped in previously,
arranged all expeditiously:
spread cushions, rugs; on couches put
comfortable weavings where they sat,   484
happy, all three, at their repast—
the girl on one side of their guest
and on the other side her sire;
in front of them a clear, bright fire.   488
     The father had no serving man
attending him at meals, save one
(or kitchen girl or serving maid);

this servant now, however, made 492
a supper of both fowl and meat
with an attention quick and neat,
soon readying all to please the host
and serving meat both boiled and roast. 496
And when he had prepared this meal
swiftly, and with dispatch and zeal,
he brought two bowls of water; brought
linen, food bowls; set tables out; 500
all was prepared, displayed, set up,
and, seated, they began to sup.
All their needs were provided for,
all their wants satisfied, and more. 504
    When they had supped at ease and then
arisen from the meal again,
Erec approached the man who was
master and holder of this house, 508
and put to him a question. "Sire,
your daughter's shabby, mean attire
distresses me. Why should she wear
such stuff? She has such savoir faire, 512
such beauty!" "Poverty, fair friend,
consorts with many. Understand,
one of her chosen troupe am I.
What shame, what pain, what agony 516
I feel to see my daughter's dress—
testament to my helplessness!
A lifetime I have been at war;
bereft of all my land and store, 520
I've pawned it, sold it; it is gone.
And here's a thought I ponder on:
Oh, I could see her so well fitted,
So well turned out, if I permitted 524

gifts from all those who volunteer!
The lord of this same castle here
would dress her—oh, noblesse oblige!
He is the count; she is his niece.   528
There is no lord in this country,
nor baron of such high degree,
he would not have my daughter's hand
on any terms I might demand.   532
But I am patient; I believe
that in his good time God will give
her greater honor. *Avanture*
will bring a count or king to her.   536
What count or king beneath the sun
need blush to have a companion
whose beauty is so rare a thing
it's new and strange, past equaling?   540
Lovely she is in any eyes,
and, more than lovely, she is wise.
Never has God before brought forth
such sweet intelligence on earth.   544
No whit I care, when she is near,
for the whole world, its hate, its fear.
Then my diversion, my delight,
solace and comfort are in sight;   548
lost wealth and treasure come again—
and her sweet self all my domain."
    Erec listened. When he had heard
all his host's story, every word,   552
he asked him then if he could say
whence came such show of chivalry
crowding inside the castle wall,
so that the poorest street was full   556
of crowds and throngs of chevaliers

and of their ladies and of squires;
no inn was thought too poor, too small.
And the host told him: "Fair friend, all   560
these are the local lords you see,
barons of this vicinity.
Youngest and oldest, whitest-haired,
all these are gathered here, prepared   564
to see tomorrow's festival.
This is why all the inns are full.
There will be great commotion here
when all the noble folk appear,   568
and before all the gathered crowd
will be a lovely sight, and proud;
a sparrow hawk upon a bar
of silver, a spectacular   572
bird, of five moltings—six, maybe.
A lovelier bird one could not see.
He who would have this hawk must have
a wise and lovely ladylove,   576
not coarse or low. If he is bold,
desires the prize, wants to uphold
his lady's fame as the most fair,
she must, while all are watching her,   580
take down the bird, claim it as hers—
if no brave rival interferes.
We have this custom every year.
That's why you see these people here."   584
     Erec put in another word.
"Fair host, I beg you, don't be bored
by all my questions. Tell me, though,
who is the knight here, do you know,   588
who goes about armed cap-a-pie,
who just now has been passing by,

bearing a crest of gold and azure,
and with him rode, for joy and pleasure, 592
close by, a girl most elegant?
And there's a hunchback dwarf in front."
His host replied: "Yes, that's the man
who will unquestionably win 596
the sparrow hawk. No contest here!
No one can bruise this chevalier!
For years now he has claimed the hawk
unchallenged, without fight or talk; 600
and if he wins again this year,
it's his own toy forevermore.
Challengers then will be too late;
there'll be no fight then or debate." 604
 Erec spoke up immediately.
"I do not like that knight," said he.
"If I had armor here with me,
I'd win that hawk! I'd make *défi*. 608
You are a noble-hearted man;
in kindness, host, say how I can
acquire some arms, I beg of you.
I don't care if they're old or new, 612
ugly, beat-up, or beautiful."
"Now, don't concern yourself at all,"
the host responded graciously.
"For I will lend you, willingly, 616
beautiful, splendid arms of mine.
A coat of woven mail, fair, fine,
I have inside. I chose it from
five hundred others. And I've some 620
shin pieces, beautiful and bright,
in mint condition, new and light.
I've a fine helmet, good and new,

and a new shield; that ought to do.   624
A charger, sword, and lance I'll give;
superior ones you could not have.
I doubt you not; have your desire."
    "Many thanks, fair and gracious sire.   628
But I do not require or crave
a sword more sturdy than I have;
I need no horse more strong or fine
or of more help to me than mine.   632
If you feel you can furnish me
with armor, that's great courtesy.
But I've another gift to ask,
which I'll repay—a cherished task—   636
if God means to allow to me
all honor and the victory."
And the host's gracious, frank response:
"Ask what you will, with confidence.   640
What is your pleasure? What I own
you will not lack; it's yours, your own."
    Now Erec speaks. He wants to claim
the hawk in his host's daughter's name,   644
for he has not seen anywhere
a girl one hundredth part as fair,
and if she bears him company,
there will be proof and certainty,   648
demonstration, beyond all talk,
she it is who deserves the hawk.
Then he says, "Sire, you have not guessed
the name or fortune of your guest,   652
his quest here or his parentage.
I'm of a great king's lineage,
the rich and puissant King Lac's son;
I am called Erec li Breton.   656

I serve King Arthur; for three years
I have served with his chevaliers;
I do not know if in this town
or in this country, the renown   660
that is my sire's, and mine, is known —
here is my promise and my boon.
If you will really lend to me
arms and your daughter's company,   664
if with your kindness, I may borrow
both and win this hawk tomorrow
— God willing! — I will take her hand,
and lead her home to my own land,   668
and make her wear the crown. And she
will have ten cities' fealty."
    "Ah, fair sire, can this be true?
Erec, the son of Lac — that's you?"   672
"Oh, absolutely! I am he."
All this the host hears joyfully.
He answers, "Much that's fine and great
we've heard of you in our small state;   676
and now I love you, prize you more,
seeing how wise and brave you are.
Nothing of mine I can refuse
to you; my daughter's yours to choose."   680
That said, he takes her by the hand:
"I give her to you, fair, sweet friend."
Erec rejoices; welcomes her;
thinks he cannot be happier.   684
    How jubilant they were, all three,
the father full of gaiety,
the mother joyous, though she wept.
The girl was calm; her spirit leapt   688
and sang to think that she should have

betrothal, and this brave man's love—
a man who would one day be king,
and she would be that honored thing,   692
a crowned queen, splendid, fair and bright.
    They stayed up almost all that night;
the waiting beds were made up, all
with white sheets, pillows, soft and full,   696
and featherbeds inviting rest.
The conversation failed at last,
and merrily they said goodnight.
    But a scant sleeper was our knight,   700
and when green dawn had thinned the sky,
then he was up immediately.
His host had risen quickly, too,
and so to church they went, these two,   704
there to entreat the Holy Ghost,
and hear the mass, and take the Host,
and watch the holy hermit sing;
neither forgot the offering.   708
Both went up to the altar, then
they returned to the house again.
    Erec was champing at the bit
now for this battle, tasting it,   712
now he is given his desire.
The girl herself serves as his squire.
No incantation, charm, or spell
she used, but laced his greaves up well   716
and tied up each deer-leather thong,
fitted the hauberk with aplomb
round him, all shining links of mail,
and then she fastened the ventail.   720
She put the helmet on his head,
and so, armed cap-a-pie, he stood.

Now at his side she belts his sword,
and he requests her, with a word, 724
to bring the horse. And with a bound,
he leaps upon it from the ground.
The firm, straight lance, the shield, she brings,
and he accepts them, takes them; hangs 728
the shield securely by its band
and takes the long lance in his hand.
Then he says to the vavasor:
"Fair sire, I ask you now: prepare 732
your daughter, for I wish to lead
her to the hawk, as we agreed."

His host had then, without delay,
a palfrey brought, a handsome bay, 736
and saddled without further fuss.
The harness we need not discuss,
the host was in such poverty
that there was no such nicety. 740
Of fancy trappings there were none.
Saddle and bridle were put on;
now mantle-less, with flowing hair,
the *pucelle* mounted, ready there; 744
no more persuasion necessary!
Now Erec did not want to tarry,
but takes his leave, and side by side
he and his good host's daughter ride, 748
and following after, nothing loath,
the father and the mother both.

He rode along, lance poised and straight,
she with him, lovely, delicate, 752
and in the streets all stopped to stare,
great folk and common, rude and rare,
wondering what this marvel was.

Whispers there were, and general buzz.   756
"Who is that? Who's that on that horse?
He must be formidably fierce
to lead a girl so beautiful;
he will employ his effort well   760
if he maintains, this chevalier,
that she's the loveliest woman here!"
And some to others: "Obviously,
the one who'll get the hawk is she!"   764
Some gave the girl such eulogies;
many spoke of his qualities.
"O Lord, who can he be, this knight,
with such a beauty at his right?"   768
"Don't know! Don't know!" the whispers swell,
"But *tiens!* He wears a helmet well!
He carries off that hauberk, too,
and shield and sword, as few men do.   772
And on that horse he looks so trim!
You see the vassal's traits in him.
Lord, but he's handsome! Stylish, neat.
He's got good arms and legs and feet."   776
    And so they gawked and whispered there,
but they did not slow down the pair,
until before the hawk they drew
and, to await their rendezvous,   780
rode to one side. And soon the knight
Erec sought rode within their sight.
Now, hear! They watched him as he came,
by him his dwarf, his high-born dame.   784
Now he, you may be sure, had heard
another knight now sought the bird.
He did not think this earth, this age
could show a knight of such courage   788

to challenge him and give him battle;
he'd flay this man, he'd make him rattle.
  All the folk knew this chevalier;
they greeted him, they bade him cheer,   792
escorting him, a noisy crowd—
sergeants and knights all boisterous, loud;
women ran after eagerly,
and girls, with great alacrity.   796
He led them, with his crumpled runt
and his *pucelle,* so elegant,
as if on a triumphal march
—but faster—toward the prize hawk's perch.   800
But the large crowd began to press
around him with great eagerness,
so densely packed, there wasn't space
to draw a crossbow in that place.   804
  Into that spot this count rode, fierce,
menacing poor folk, commoners—
he waved a switch and threatened them,
though they came crowding after him   808
spoke to his girl, before the hawk,
and smooth and tranquil was his talk:
"This bird, my dear, my demoiselle,
lovely, you see, and mewed so well,   812
now, by all rights, belongs to you,
beautiful girl; it is your due,
your prize, until my own life's end.
Take it; come here, my fair, sweet friend.   816
Move from its perch this hawk, my gift."
  The girl reached forth her hand, to lift
the bird down. But now Erec ran
heedless of her desire and plan.   820
"Damsel," he said, "away! Stand back!

You'll have to find another hawk,
for you've no right to this one here.
Save yourself grief; leave off, my dear.   824
The prize bird never can be yours;
a better girl will make it hers—
a lovelier girl, more courteous."
    The other knight was furious;   828
Erec thought that of little worth.
He urged his own girl to come forth.
"Beauty," he said, "come forward now.
Take down the bird from off its bough.   832
For it is only right and fair
that it be yours. Come! Claim it here,
I will support you. I'll stand by
against all comers who may try—   836
none can prevail against you, none.
The moon cannot outshine the sun;
Your beauty, worth, and grace are such
as rivals cannot hope to touch."   840
    The big knight heard these urgings and
now had as much as he could stand;
and so, provoked, he took his cue:
"Who," he said, "vassal, who are you,   844
who claims our hawk on such a whim?"
And Erec firmly answered him:
"A knight from another country, who
has come to seek this hawk, as due   848
this lady. Her right's obvious.
Bad luck, sir knight! Accept your loss!"
"Never! Move off! Go, go! Away!
—or else keep on this course. You'll pay,   852
dearly, but try the hawk. You'll see
the price of your stupidity."

"I'll pay? Well, vassal, tell me how."
"Attempt to battle with me now,   856
or drop your claim, so poor and weak."
"Lunatic posturings you speak,"
said Erec. "Lord, the threats he brings!
The sweet and airy menacings!   860
Somehow my fears seem small to me."
"Then take my challenge, instantly:
it seems there must be battle here."
"God help me," said our chevalier,   864
"I wish that more than anything."
Now you shall hear those lances ring.
     The field, now cleared, was spacious, wide,
and people stood on every side,   868
more than an acre, now, these two
back off before their rendezvous
and rush together on their course.
The lance heads crack with vicious force,   872
the clattering shields are pierced and battered,
the lances dashed to bits and shattered
The saddlebows break up and smash,
feet leave their stirrups with a crash—   876
both fall to earth; their stirrups yield.
The horses tear across the field.
     The men leap up. Their lances gone
—used to good purpose—they fight on.   880
Each from his scabbard draws his sword
and with ferocious, cruel accord
they hew and prune and carve; they make
the helmets sing and crack and break.   884
Furiously these two irons meet,
on necks and shoulders slash and beat;
no hesitations haunt these men.

They harrow, tear, and strike again,   888
batter the shields; attack, and smash
the bright linked hauberks. As they slash,
the swords are stained with scarlet blood.
　　The fight lasts long; in fiercer mood   892
they strive, exhausted now, and worn.
Each lady weeps; and each man, torn,
sees his friend's tears, her frantic prayer,
hands clenched, that God hear now and care,   896
grant victory to her chevalier,
who labors now and bleeds for her.
"Vassal," now spoke that other knight,
"let us draw back for some respite   900
and give ourselves a bit of rest.
Our blows are weak; we've lost our zest.
We must deliver better blows;
evening will soon be here, God knows.   904
It's shameful and embarrassing
how long we have been battling.
Let's pause, for our friends' sakes, and then,
fighting our best, cross swords again."   908
"Good!" said Erec. They rested. There
he saw his frightened girl at prayer,
And as he watched his new-found love,
he felt his courage stir and move   912
and gather force. Now her concern,
her love, her beauty, made him burn
with pride. He thought of Guinevere,
how in the woods he'd promised her   916
he would avenge her insult or
make it more heinous than before.
　　"Ha! I'm a sorry sort, and poor,"
he said. "What am I waiting for?   920

I haven't yet avenged the slight,
so crude, permitted by this knight,
when his dwarf struck me in the glade."
His anger heightened, and he said   924
furiously to the chevalier:
"Come at once, sire! I call you here!
This rest is wasting half the day.
To battle! Back to swords and play!"   928
"To it! I feel no grief at that,"
the other said. And so they fought.
    Both set to, fencing furiously,
and Erec parried skillfully,   932
avoiding thus a vicious wound,
for his opponent's sword cut round
under his shield and hacked away
part of his helmet, to display   936
gleaming and bare, the skull-tight coif,
and, still descending, splintered off
the shield, down to the buckle, then
sliced through the hauberk, where, again,   940
it bit the bright chain mail and tore
open the side a span or more.
Now here was trouble; on his side,
bare flesh, he felt the bright sword glide,   944
he felt the cold steel on his thigh.
Now this time God watched from on high,
for if one turn had then been made
with that cold sword, he'd have been flayed;   948
but Erec, not at all dismayed,
said that his debt was well repaid.
Boldly he struck and hacked and frayed
his adversary's shoulder blade,   952
dealing such force upon the shield

it would not hold up, but must yield.
The hauberk failed; the bright links gone,
the sword bit almost to the bone.   956
In scarlet rivulets blood gushed
and to the waistband steamed and rushed.
Now with more fierce intensity
they battled, matched so equally   960
that neither vassal seemed to put
his foe back by a single foot.
   Shredded the hauberks were, and stripped,
and the shields torn in chunks and ripped,   964
not whole enough, I do not lie
to guard against an enemy.
Both hack away, and flesh expose;
masses of blood they've lost; their blows   968
have made them weak in every limb.
The knight strikes Erec; Erec him,
delivering a blow he feels
full on the helmet, so he reels.   972
Again, again, with fierce, free joy,
Erec strikes, three times, vigorously.
Now into quarters he hacks and breaks
the helmet, and the coif he rakes   976
and tears; the sword, though, does not pause
just at the head, but cuts and saws
into the skull, yet spares the brain.
The other falters, starts to lean,   980
tottering. Then Erec pushes;
on his right side the other crashes;
the helmet Erec takes, to pull
it roughly, harshly, from the skull;   984
starts, then, the ventail to unlace,
uncovers all the head and face.

When he thinks of the vicious scene,
the dwarf's outrage upon the queen,   988
he thinks to cut the knight's head off,
but "Mercy!" the other cries. "Enough!
Vassal, you've won; you've vanquished me.
Don't kill me; show some clemency.   992
Now you've prevailed and taken me;
what prize, what honor, can there be
in slaying me? Sir knight, take heed;
you will have done a vicious deed.   996
Here is my sword; take it, I pray."
Erec declined it courteously.
"Good. I won't kill you; do not fear."
"Thanks to you, noble chevalier!   1000
But what offense, what injury,
has earned this deadly enmity?
I don't think I've laid eyes on you;
What wrong or insult could I do?   1004
What slur to honor? Vassal, none!"
And Erec said, "Just that you've done."
"Well! Fair sire, tell me it then!
If I've seen you, I don't know when;   1008
if I have injured you before,
mercy, I beg! Sire, I implore!"
Erec said, "Vassal, I am he
whom you saw ride in company   1012
yesterday with Queen Guinevere,
where you allowed, it would appear,
your dwarf to strike the queen's own maid.
What villainy the oaf displayed,   1016
striking a woman! He struck me,
and you assessed me, obviously,
as some low churl. The outrage, yours!

Watching an outrage like this boor's,   1020
you aided and abetted it
from that abortion, that misfit,
that shrimp, who lashed the girl and me.
For this I hate you cordially—   1024
you, your excessive contumely!
Now you're my prisoner; swear to me,
that without wandering and delay,
you'll seek my lady straightaway.   1028
You'll find her—without fail you can—
if you now go to Cardigan.
Indeed you can arrive today;
it isn't seven leagues away.   1032
You and your dwarf and your *pucelle*
you will present to her as well;
you will deliver to her hand
all three, to be at her command.   1036
And you'll convey this word for me:
I'll come tomorrow, joyfully,
leading a girl so wise, so fair,
distinguished, full of savoir faire,   1040
they'll see and say in this affair
she has no equal anywhere.
And now, sir knight, tell me your name."
     Having no choice, the man was game.   1044
"I am called Yder, son of Nut.
This morning I could not have thought
that any man by chivalry
could overpower and vanquish me.   1048
I've found a better man; no doubt
he's proved himself and found me out.
You are a valiant knight, that's sure.

Accept my promise; I do swear   1052
to seek your queen without delay.
But you must tell me, you must say
your name, and not keep secrecy.
Who shall I say commanded me?   1056
Speak, tell me; I'll be on my way."
    The other said: "I'll gladly say,
I'll not conceal it. You must know,
I am called Erec. When you go,   1060
tell her I've sent you. Now, be off."
"I shall oblige you. I, my dwarf,
and maid shall go to Guinevere,
we'll ask her mercy, never fear,   1064
and certainly, fair sire, we'll tell
the news of you and your *pucelle*."
Erec received the vassal's word.
    This parting all the folk had heard,   1068
the count and all his entourage,
maidens and lords of his menage.
Some felt chagrin, and some delight;
Some felt weighed down, and some felt light;   1072
and for the girl in shabby white,
noble in heart and thought and sight,
the daughter of the vavasor,
most felt great gladness and pleasure.   1076
But some felt sadness for Yder,
who loved him and his lady fair.
    Yder was anxious now to go
acquit himself without ado;   1080
and now he leaped upon his horse.
Why make this tale laborious?
Now with his dwarf and his *pucelle*

he rode through forest, plain, and fell,   1084
and straight along the way they ran
until they came to Cardigan.

ON THE GREAT hall's high gallery
Sir Gawain stood; with him Sir Kay,   1088
who was King Arthur's seneschal.
And also many barons; all
had followed them, it seems to me.
And now our travelers, all three,   1092
were well observed. It was Sir Kay
who saw them first and turned to say
to Gawain: "My heart hints to me,
fair sire, this vassal whom we see   1096
is just the one who yesterday
the queen says caused her such dismay.
It's my suspicion it's these three;
I see the dwarf and the lady."   1100
    "Yes, I see too," said Sir Gawain.
"Lady and dwarf it is: that's plain.
There they are with the chevalier,
moving with haste toward us here.   1104
That knight is armed from head to feet;
surely his shield looks incomplete.
If the queen sees this caravan,
I think she'll recognize the man.   1108
Ho! Seneschal! Ask her! Go see!"
    Sir Kay went off immediately,
and found her in her room. "Lady,
can you call up in memory   1112
a dwarf who angered you, you say,

and whipped your handmaid, yesterday?"
"Indeed, I certainly recall.
Do you know something, seneschal?   1116
Why do you ask me?" said the queen.
"Lady, because just now I've seen
a knight-errant who comes this way,
armed, on a charger, iron gray.   1120
Unless my eyes play tricks on me,
a girl he has in company,
and with his whip, the small fellow
who gave Erec that dastard blow."   1124
    The queen got up at once. "Let's go
now, seneschal; I want to know
whether the vassal you've on hand
was in that hateful little band.   1128
You may be sure that I can tell
if it's that vassal — very well,
as soon as I lay eyes on him."
And Kay replied: "I'll lead you, then.   1132
Come with me to the lodge, fair friend,
where our companions all attend
this band they've seen. There Sir Gawain
himself awaits you. Come, it's plain   1136
we've idled. There's no time to waste."
    The queen bestirred herself, with haste.
Up to the windows now she came
and placed herself by Sir Gawain.   1140
Immediately she knew the knight.
"Ha!" she said. "Oh, that's him, all right.
He's been in danger; some great fight.
He's very battered — put to flight,   1144
perhaps? Erec has dealt him this?
—Or he's been Erec's nemesis.

His shield, I see, is full of blows,
his hauberk full of blood. It shows   1148
not so much white as it does red."
    "I see it does," Sir Gawain said.
"My lady, I am very sure
you've lied in no particular.   1152
His hauberk's bloody, pounded, bent,
and much abused; it's evident
he's been in combat, and for sure
he bears about him marks of war.   1156
We shall determine, without fail,
whose strength it was that could prevail—
whether Erec has sent him here
as his own vanquished prisoner,   1160
craving our mercy; or, by chance,
full of insensate arrogance,
with Erec killed or overthrown,
he comes to make his triumph known.   1164
I think he brings no news but this."
    "I think so too," the queen says. "Yes,
it may well be," the others state.
    Yder now enters through the gate,   1168
bearing the news they've wanted so.
And from the loge they turn to go;
they hurry down, each chevalier,
anxious to see, to know, to hear;   1172
they come below, to meet Yder,
who waits just at the bottom stair.
Yder dismounts; and Sir Gawain
lifts up the lady, sets her down;   1176
the dwarf gets off his animal.
A hundred knights there are in all,
or more. Now, quickly gathering,

they take the three before the king.   1180
    Yder now sees Queen Guinevere,
and rushes quickly up to her,
falls at her feet. First, though, by rights,
he greets King Arthur and the knights,   1184
and then he speaks to Guinevere.
"My lady, as your prisoner
I here present myself: one sent
by a most virtuous, excellent   1188
and worthy knight, who yesterday
felt my dwarf's whip in vicious play.
This knight has conquered, vanquished me;
here I conduct my dwarf, you see,   1192
and my own lady. Our behest:
do with us now as you think best."
    When he had made this speech, she broke
her silence, asked for news, and spoke   1196
of Erec. "Now, sire, say to me,
is Erec coming presently?"
"Lady, tomorrow, he will come.
And there's a damsel rides with him,   1200
the loveliest I have ever seen."
    When she had heard this news, the queen
spoke tactfully and graciously.
"Friend," she addressed him, courteously,   1204
"since you come as my prisoner,
you'll have much milder sentence here;
I wish you no harm, certainly.
So help you God, now say to me,   1208
what is your name?" He said to her:
"I am the son of Nut, Yder."
    This truth they could all recognize.
Now the queen rose, before all eyes,   1212

to see the king. Said Guinevere:
"You've heard? How well advised you were
to wait for our brave chevalier,
our Erec, to at last appear.   1216
You had good counsel, sire, from me.
Observe what profit there can be
from taking others' good advice."
"Lady," he said, "you speak no lies.   1220
Your words are truth, and they must rule.
He who takes counsel is no fool.
But if you love me as you say,
let this knight be quit straightaway   1224
of his imprisonment and vows.
Let him be henceforth of our house,
part of our menage, court, and hall;
his loss, if he refuse us all."   1228
    The king no sooner spoke, than she
absolved Yder and set him free,
with all due form and cherished rite.
With this provision: that the knight   1232
must stay at Arthur's court and hall.
He needed urging not at all,
but gave his promise. Now, in short,
he sojourned there at Arthur's court.   1236
Hardly had Sir Yder agreed
when valets, hurrying to his need,
came to relieve him of his arms.

Now to Erec the tale returns,   1240
still at the scene of battle, where
he had just overcome Yder.

Never, I think, was such joy felt
since Tristan fought and killed Morholt, 1244
vanquishing him on Saint-Samson;
such was the joy of everyone.
Much honor now was Erec's lot;
from small and great, from lank and fat, 1248
all prized, all praised, his chivalry.
There was no knight who did not say:
"God! Under heaven there's no such man!"
    And afterward, when he had gone 1252
back to his hostel, he was shown
great praise, fair speech, by everyone.
The count himself embraced his neck,
made joyous welcome for Erec, 1256
said, "Reason, my fair sire, allows
you take your lodging at my house,
since you are King Lac's son. Say yes:
if you accept my services, 1260
I shall be greatly honored, for
you are — most surely — my seignior.
I crave your grace in this. Sire, do:
remain with me, I beg of you." 1264
    "Do not be vexed," then said our knight.
"I will not leave my host this night.
To me he has great honor shown:
given his daughter for my own. 1268
What say you of this present, sire?
What present thoughts does it inspire?
Is it not rich and lovely?" "Yes,
fair sire: lovely and rich it is. 1272
She is wise, fair, and virtuous,
her lineage high and glorious.
You make my heart rejoice. You know,

her mother is my sister; so,   1276
fair sire, you deign to have my niece.
Again, I must beseech you: please,
come tonight. Let my house provide."
"Leave me in peace," Erec replied.   1280
"For all the world, I will not go."
    The count saw he would have it so,
with no more prayers. "Sire, as you please.
Now we will silence all our pleas.   1284
But I and all my knights shall come
and lodge ourselves as you have done,
for cheer and for good company."
Erec received this courtesy,   1288
and then he went to seek his host.
Beside him rode the count; his host
of knights and ladies he had there.
They made great joy; they made great cheer.   1292
    And now Erec returns, he's come,
and sergeants—more than twenty—run
and take his armor straightaway.
Those of the house rejoice, display   1296
—most ably—cheer at seeing him.
Erec is seated first, and then,
by rank, the others, as is fit:
on benches, couches, stools, they sit.   1300
There is the count, beside our knight—
but in between, the girl in white,
who has such joy in her seignior.
Never has any girl had more.   1304
    Erec now called the vavasor.
Lovely and generous words these were.
Thus he began his speech, to state:
"Fair friend, fair host, fair sire, a great   1308

honor to me you've given and shown:
you shall be well repaid in turn.
Tomorrow I shall go and bring
your daughter to the court and king;   1312
there I desire to marry her.
You — if it pleases you — wait here,
a little while, until I send
for you and lead you to my land,   1316
where my sire rules — and so shall I.
It's far from here; it's not close by.
Once you are there, I shall bestow
on you two splendid, fair châteaus.   1320
One of these is called Roadan,
built in the time of the first man.
The other's very close to it,
and no less splendid, not one whit.   1324
Montrevel people call this one.
My father has no better — none.
After the first three days go by
I shall send you a fair supply   1328
of gold and silver, squirrel and vair,
and silken stuffs, most dear, most rare,
for you and for your wife to wear,
for she's my sweet prized lady fair.   1332
Tomorrow, at the crack of dawn,
in that same dress, in that same gown,
I'll lead your daughter, I'll escort
her with me to King Arthur's court.   1336
I wish my lady Guinevere
there to bestow a gown on her,
her silken gown of scarlet dye."
    There was a girl who sat nearby;   1340
shrewd, wise, she'd many a social gift.

Next to the girl in the white shift
upon a bench this damsel sat.
She was her cousin; beside that,   1344
the count's own niece. She spoke to him.
"Sire," she now told him, "much chagrin
you'll have, and others will have, too,
if this lord, as he means to do,   1348
leads off your niece, dressed as she is,
attired in such a gown as this."
The count replied: "I beg you, niece,
sweet one, that you will give her, please,   1352
of all the gowns you have, the best,
the richest and the loveliest."
　　All this discussion Erec heard.
"Sire," he said, "not another word.   1356
Be sure you understand one thing:
no dress I wish you now to bring,
no gown I wish for her to wear,
but that the queen will give to her."   1360
The damsel heard this firm decree,
and then she answered him. "*Haï!*
Fair sire, since in this style you please
in her white shift and her chemise   1364
to lead my cousin forth in love,
another gift I wish to give.
Since your desire is absolute
and none of my attire will suit,   1368
I have three palfreys, lovely mounts
—kings have not better ones, nor counts—
sorrel and white-foot, dapple gray.
It is no lie for me to say   1372
among a hundred steeds, this last
would certainly not be surpassed.
The birds that dart about the air

are not more swift than this same vair, 1376
no man has seen his faults as yet.
A child could ride him, and he's fit,
ideally, for a girl to ride.
He does not kick; he does not bite; 1380
he's never skittish, restive, shy,
nor violent in any way.
Who seeks a better has no sense
of what it is he really wants. 1384
Carefree he'll fare, and easily,
as if a ship he rode, at sea."
    "My fair, sweet friend," Erec replied,
"I would not have this gift denied, 1388
if she will take it. Let me state,
I hope that she'll not hesitate."
And now the damsel calls to her
her sergeant, her own follower, 1392
and says to him: "My fair friend, go,
saddle my dappled palfrey now
and lead him here immediately."
And he went expeditiously, 1396
and made much fuss, and took much pain,
saddled the horse with flowing mane,
and then he rode the palfrey out.
Erec assessed it; without doubt 1400
his praise was neither faint nor small.
He thought it a fine animal,
gentle and beautiful withal.
A sergeant led it to the stall 1404
where his own charger had been led.
Next to it now, the palfrey's bed.
    Now to their beds the guests all went;
this night they'd had great merriment. 1408
The count went to his house once more,

left Erec with the vavasor,
and said he'd bear him company
next morning, when he went his way.　　　　1412
　　All of the folk slept well that night.
When dawn had thinned the sky with light,
Erec arose and made his plans,
had his horse saddled, gave commands.　　　　1416
And she awoke, his fair *amie*,
rose, dressed herself, and made ready;
the vavasor, his wife, arose.
No knight or lady there but chose　　　　1420
to up and ride, and to convey
this knight and maiden on their way.
All of them gather; now they mount,
and Erec rides beside the count,　　　　1424
beside him, too, his lady fair,
who has her sparrow hawk with her.
She humors it and strokes it, plays;
bears no more riches from that place.　　　　1428
　　Great joy these escorts have at heart;
the noble count seeks, when they part,
to send a smaller embassy,
for honor and for courtesy.　　　　1432
But Erec asks that they not stay.
No company along the way
he wants, but that of his *amie*.
"To God I commend you," then says he.　　　　1436
　　They'd ridden far, a lengthy piece.
The count kissed Erec and his niece,
commended them to God's mercy;
father and mother earnestly　　　　1440
kissed the girl often, made great fuss,
and, oh, the tears were copious!

How at this parting wept the mother,
father and daughter, all together!   1444
Well, love is like that; so is nature,
so is the pity bred by nurture.
They wept for pity and for love,
that tenderness that people have   1448
for offspring; but they knew, however,
that where their child went with her lover
for them great honor would accrue.
And so they wept to see her go,   1452
for nothing else but tenderness;
since, after all, this pair could guess
what honor would be theirs, for sure.
Thus they wept at her departure,   1456
and to God each commended each;
they left, then, without further speech.
    And Erec parted from his host,
anxious, for precious time was lost.   1460
Soon he must be at Arthur's court.
But in this *avanture* was brought
such happiness, such joy and glee!
How beautiful was his *amie,*   1464
how courteous, wise, and debonair!
Now he can't cease to look at her,
again, again; cannot resist
the gentle pressure of a kiss;   1468
willingly he draws near to her,
restored in spirit, full of cheer.
Much he admires her golden head,
her laughing eyes, her bright forehead,   1472
her features, nose and mouth and face;
they touch his heart with a sweet grace.
Down to her hips he steals a glance,

at her white throat, her chin, her hands,   1476
her lovely arms, her flanks, her side.
And she, too, glances; on her side
feels no less drawn; the demoiselle
admires the vassal, knowing well   1480
his good intent, his loyal heart,
and in her looks she does her part
in this new contest now at stake.
No ransom would these lovers take   1484
to leave off all these looks they share.
Equal they are, an ideal pair,
in beauty and in courtesy,
in goodness and nobility.   1488
In manners, ways, and character,
and nature, they are similar;
so much so, that one could not say
or choose the better, possibly—   1492
the lovelier, wiser, more discreet.
Their kindred spirits seem to meet,
accommodating joyfully;
each steals the other's heart away.   1496
Two fairer pictures of our kind
marriage or law have never joined.
    And so they rode together. Soon,
when it was getting on for noon,   1500
they approached Castle Cardigan,
awaited, both, by everyone.

૮ꝑ૪

TO WATCH FOR them as they drew near,
chief barons, each a powerful peer,   1504
had mounted to the windows there.

And with them ran Queen Guinevere;
the king himself, and Sir Kay, ran;
Perceval, the Welsh nobleman;   1508
Sir Gawain, too, was in the chase,
and Cortz, the son of King Ares;
Lucan, the royal cupbearer,
and many a noble chevalier.   1512
    Now as they watched, they all could see
Erec ride, leading his *amie*.
How jubilant was Guinevere!
The court was full of joy and cheer,   1516
as they stood watching this event,
so much their love for Erec meant.
Just as he rode before the hall,
the king descended first of all,   1520
and the queen hastened, from her side.
"God save you!" all the courtiers cried.
Welcome they gave to his fair guest,
and much they praised her loveliness;   1524
he, the king, seized her, raised her, then
set her down from her horse again.
Nothing if not well-bred was he,
and just now full of gaiety,   1528
and with great honor, then and there,
by the hand led her up the stair,
where the main hall, of stone, was found.
After them mounted, hand in hand,   1532
Erec and the Queen Guinevere.
    "Lady," he said, "I bring you here
my damsel, and my own *amie*,
dressed in poor garments, as you see.   1536
Just as the girl was given to me,
I lead her to you, joyfully,

the daughter of a vavasor,
a man brought low, as many are,   1540
by poverty; but courteous,
though of small means, and piteous.
As gentle as you'd wish, her mother;
and, gentle, too, the count, her brother.   1544
Not for her beauty, nor estate,
nor lineage, should I hesitate
to take to wife this demoiselle.
Poverty and sheer want compel   1548
her wearing of this white chemise,
worn through the elbows of both sleeves.
If it had been my wish, she could
have gowns enough, both fair and good,   1552
for her own cousin offered her
a splendid dress of ermine fur,
of silken stuff, or squirrel, or vair.
I did not wish to see her wear   1556
the sort of dress one would prefer
until you had laid eyes on her.
My sweet queen, think, and counsel me,
for she has need, you surely see,   1560
of a fine, fitting dress to wear."
    Then said at once Queen Guinevere:
"Well said, my dear sire, and well done.
Fitting it is that she have one   1564
of my own gowns, one good and fair—
fitting to her, fitting to wear
immediately, all fresh and new."
    She led the girl, without ado,   1568
to her own chamber and had brought
immediately a fresh *bliaut,*
a mantle, and a dress all sewn

with little crosses — new, her own.   1572
She who had been commanded brought
just such a mantle as they sought;
with it an ermine white *bliaut,*
furred to the sleeves, and at the throat,   1576
or neckband, and the wrists there lay
a marvel, without sorcery —
two hundred marks of beaten gold,
or more, and stones of price untold   1580
—dark blue, dark brown, green, violet
all in fine gold these gems were set.
Splendid and rich this tunic was,
but surely no less sumptuous   1584
the mantle, rich to look upon.
Ribbons had not yet been put on,
for all these clothes were fresh and new,
the *bliaut* and the mantle too.   1588
Splendid the mantle, a rich coat
of sable skins just at the throat;
a gold ounce in each tassel shone.
A hyacinth, a dark blue stone,   1592
graced one side, and a ruby, sole,
and brighter than a reddened coal,
was on the other. Beneath all,
a lining there was, beautiful,   1596
of ermine, deep and thick and white.
One could not find a lovelier sight.
The cloth was worked most wonderfully
in crosslets, a variety,   1600
green, white, vermilion, yellow hues,
violet, azure, deeper blues;
five ells of ribbon, threaded, wrought
with silk and gold the queen had brought,   1604

and brought they were, with much dispatch,
splendid, all ready to attach.
Attached they were, immediately;
the queen at once, without delay,   1608
sent for a man whose craft and wit
enabled him to finish it.
    Finished it was, and fit to wear.
The noble queen, so debonair,   1612
summoned the girl in her white shift,
spoke noble words, bestowed her gift;
"My demoiselle, this *bliaut* here
is worth a hundred marks or more   1616
of silver. I command you, then:
Leave now that shift, and put this on.
So I would honor you. And don
this mantle over all; anon   1620
you shall have other gifts from me."
What hesitation could there be?
The girl gave thanks; she took the gown.
    Now to a hidden little room   1624
two maidens lead her; there, at ease,
the girl casts off her old chemise.
On goes the *bliaut* in its place,
with the rich belt of golden lace,   1628
and the poor shift is given away,
for love of God, to charity.
The mantle goes on last of all.
No sight to make the spirits pall,   1632
this figure; how these clothes become her!
How her own beauty does them honor!
Now the two girls take threads of gold,
and through her locks they plait and fold   1636
the shining wire, but her own hair

is far more brilliant, far more fair,
than the fine metal. On her head
a golden circlet then is laid,   1640
intricately wrought with flowers
of many deep and glowing colors.
They do their best, adorning her;
Their work is faultless, to be sure.   1644
Two niello clasps, then, black and gold,
a topaz has been made to hold
one girl puts round her neck as well.
So comely is the demoiselle,   1648
so charming, that you could not find
in any country, to my mind,
search as you might, her equal there.
Nature worked well in this affair.   1652
    Out of the chamber where she's been
she comes, adorned to see the queen.
The queen rejoices in the sight;
she loves the girl, and takes delight   1656
in one so courteous and so fair.
Now they take hands, and they repair,
thus linked, to see the king once more.
And the king, when he sees them there,   1660
arises, meets them where they stand.
So many knights there were on hand,
who, as they came into the room,
rose, and immediately welcomed them.   1664
A tenth of these I could not name,
a thirteenth, fifteenth; but the fame
of some was great, and the chief lords
I'll name for you, I'll speak the words,   1668
all men of the Round Table's worth—
there were no better knights on earth.

Of these good knights, the first and best
was Gawain; he led all the rest.   1672
Second was Erec, son of Lac;
and the third, Lancelot du Lac;
and Gonemanz de Goort was fourth;
fifth, the Handsome Coward stepped forth.   1676
The sixth was Mean-and-Ugly Bold;
seventh, Melianz des Liz, I'm told;
eighth, Maudiz the Wise—and good;
ninth, Dodins the Wild—and rude;   1680
the tenth I'll mention, Gaudeluz:
his was a soul that bore sweet fruits.
Now no more numbers shall I say;
they bore me and get in my way.   1684
Yvain the Valiant sat quite near
Yvain the Bastard. Also there,
Tristan who never laughed, and this
knight sat beside Blioberis.   1688
Caradué Briebraz was there,
that skillful, helpful succorer,
and Caverons de Roberdic,
and then the son of Quenedic,   1692
the vassal of Quintareus,
Ydiers of the Mount Dolorous,
Galeriez and Quex d'Estraus,
Amauguins and Galez li Chaus,   1696
Gilflez, Do's son, and then Taulas—
Oh, never tired of arms, he was!
A vassal of great worthiness,
Loholz, King Arthur's son, no less,   1700
and Sagremors le Dezreez—
Oh, not a man whom one forgets!
Nor should Bedoiers, the constable,

who so loved chess and games at table,   1704
nor Bravains, nor, of course, King Lot,
nor Galegantin be forgot.
    When the enchanting foreigner
saw all these knights regarding her   1708
with acute interest, steadfastly,
she bowed her head, confusedly,
and, not surprisingly, she blushed.
Vermilion was her face, all flushed,   1712
with shame and shyness. Who could blame her?
But it most wonderfully became her.
    When the king saw her troubled state,
her blush, he did not hesitate,   1716
but gently took her hand, in sight
of all, and set her at his right.
Now at his left sat Guinevere,
who said with grace and courtly cheer: 1720
"Sire, it is fitting, I believe,
that at the king's court we receive
a knight whose feats could win so well
on foreign soil, so beautiful   1724
a girl. Oh, we did well to wait
for Erec; it's appropriate
that now you take the kiss from her
who is most comely and most fair.   1728
No one will take the deed amiss
or say I lie. I say this kiss
is for this lady, loveliest,
noblest, most courteous and best   1732
of all the maidens gathered here.
No girl on earth is lovelier."
    The king replied: "That is no lie.
This girl, if no one will deny   1736

or challenge me, I'll give the kiss."
And to the knights, the king said this:
"How say you, lords? What's your decree?
This body and this face you see,   1740
these proper graces. Knights, is she
best, loveliest? First in courtesy?
She has no peer, it seems to me,
where the earth joins the canopy   1744
of heaven. I think it not amiss
this honor should be hers, this kiss.
But you, my lords, what will you say?
Will you contend with me? Say nay?   1748
If you've another cause to plead,
speak up, speak freely. We shall heed.
I am the king; and I must see
no lies prevail, no villainy,   1752
deception, or immoderate claims.
I must guard reason, right; the aims
appropriate to a loyal king:
maintain the law, thus nurturing   1756
truth, faith, and justice. These I prize;
I would not have in any guise
disloyalty, betrayal, wrong—
not for the weak or for the strong.   1760
Here I must have no man complain.
And my desire is to maintain
those customs, usages, and just
laws that my forebears held in trust.   1764
It would distress you much, I know,
were I to introduce to you
other observances and laws
than those my forebears made their cause.   1768
The usages that heretofore

were those of king and emperor,
of Uther Pendragon, my sire,
I shall maintain. That's my desire   1772
while I have power. Now you must state
your wishes; speak, don't hesitate.
Shall this fair girl, this lovely wight
—not of our house—by all that's right   1776
receive the ceremonial kiss?
Tell me, my lords, the truth of this."
    They spoke; they answered with one voice.
"By God and by His Cross, the choice   1780
is yours. You can make judgment best
whether this girl is loveliest.
She has more beauty, in our sight,
than the sun has effulgent light.   1784
Give her the kiss; and be assured
you have our firm, communal word."
    So spoke the knights; and Arthur heard.
He did not linger, but concurred,   1788
gave her the kiss most courteously,
before the barons. Then said he:
"My fair, sweet friend, I gladly prove
without base thoughts or deeds, my love: 1792
and I will love you, with good will,
with no deception, or evil."
By this adventure, watched by all,
Arthur fulfilled the ritual;   1796
now the old custom could prevail.
    Here ends the first part of this tale.

ARTHUR HAD DONE his office now,
carried out custom and his vow.   1800
Erec, a man of courtesy,
now thought of his host's poverty,
and his own promises. No lies
or failures must result from these.   1804
Now he made good his word; said he
was sending on immediately
five fat and healthy sumpter mules,
laden with garments: fabrics, wools,   1808
buckrams, the silk called *escarlate,*
and coins—gold marks—and silver plate,
and all the loveliest, fairest fur,
sable and vair and miniver;   1812
rich stuffs; the silk called *osterin.*
With all that suits a nobleman
the mules were heaped; beside them, ten
chevaliers and ten sergeants, men   1816
of Erec's house, led all away.
He gave these counsel urgently:
they must show honor, reverence,
salute his host with deference   1820
like that due Erec personally.
When they'd been given, faithfully,
the mules and all their store and sum,
golden coins of Byzantium,   1824
silver and gold and rich array,
from all these trunks, without delay
they would be led to Estre-Gales,
Erec's own kingdom. To its palace   1828
they would be led, in all accord
and all due honor, dame and lord.
Two castles were in this bequest:

they were the realm's two loveliest 1832
and best; their strength superior,
they had least cause to fear a war.
Montrevel was the name of one;
the other was called Roadan. 1836
Once in the kingdom, they'd receive
two strongholds, where the pair would live.
They'd have delivered for their needs
rents, rights of justice, charters, deeds. 1840
  Silver and gold and shining wares,
rich garments, gleaming deniers
—things of which Erec had a host—
were now delivered to his host, 1844
sent by his messengers that day;
they had no reason to delay.
To Erec's kingdom, then, they bore
the old dame and the vavasor; 1848
this with much honor and much praise.
They reached the country in three days,
received each castle, keep, and tower.
King Lac did all within his power 1852
to honor them and undertake
to love them both for Erec's sake.
The keeps were ceded over, both;
surety made, and vow and oath. 1856
Each bourgeois and each chevalier
swore to be loyal and hold dear
this couple, as their rightful lords.
When cherished customs and fair words 1860
had been observed, then Erec's men
made their way back to him again.
Erec received them, with good cheer,
inquired most eagerly, to hear 1864

of realm, sire, dame, and vavasor;
All of this news was good and fair.

ALMOST WITH NO delay at all,
the day arrived for the nuptial   1868
observance, set some time before.
Erec found waiting painful, for
endurance, patience, and denial
were not what he was best at. While   1872
chafing, he went to see his liege,
and asked of him a privilege:
could this marriage be held at court?
Willingly Arthur gave support   1876
to this request. The king sought out
kings, dukes, and counts; he said, throughout
his kingdom, each must be his guest
at this great feast of Pentecost.   1880
No one would dare remain at home,
or be so bold as not to come,
if he required them to be there.
    Listen to me! I will declare   1884
the kings and counts in that entourage,
each splendid, lordly equipage.
Branles of Colchester, who led
just at his right, a hundred head   1888
of horses; and Menagormon,
who was the lord of Eglimon;
The Man of the High Mountain, then,
with all his splendid noblemen;   1892
and then the count of Traverain —
a hundred knights there, to a man.

Count Godegrains was next, and he
had no less in his company;   1896
and I must mention Moloas,
a rich, brave warrior, who was
lord of the [Glass] Isle, where they fear
no thunder, ever, nor need fear   1900
the lightning's strike or death by storm.
There lives no toad, nor snake, nor worm;
weather's not wintry, nor too warm.
There was Greslemenf d'Estre Posterne   1904
with twenty of his warriors,
also his brother, Guingamars,
who was the lord of Avalon.
He had been the *ami,* this man,   1908
of Morgan la Fée—so I have heard.
This is proved fact, not idle word.
David, from Tintagel, came too;
This man did not know rage or woe.   1912
       Counts and dukes were in evidence;
kings came in real magnificence.
First, the fierce king of Cork, Garraz,
with his five hundred knights; there was   1916
a shimmering, brilliant crew, for all
wore cloaks and tunics of sendal,
sleeves and hose that whispered and shone.
Aguiflez, who held the throne   1920
of Scotland, came; he led his sons
Cadret and Quoi, three dreaded ones;
he rode a Cappadocian horse.
Others I must name in due course;   1924
there was King Bans of Ganieret,
and with him there a company
of boys; for, as it soon appeared,

none had a mustache or a beard.   1928
A noisy, jolly entourage!
Two hundred were in this menage.
Each on his wrist bore, on display,
a falcon or some bird of prey: 1932
merlin or sparrow hawk, or here
a yearling bird or a crane catcher.
Quirions of Orcel, elderly,
had no young men in company,   1936
two hundred came with him, all told;
the youngest a mere century old.
Now all had, in this entourage,
white, snowy hair, the gift of age;   1940
their beards reached to their belts. They were
dearly loved by the king, Arthur.
Then the king of the dwarfs, Bilis,
monarch of the Antipodes;   1944
a dwarf himself, he had his giant
brother with him, a man named Bliant.
Of all the dwarfs Bilis was smallest,
and his brother Bliant was tallest   1948
by half a foot, or a whole hand,
of any man in Arthur's land.
For show and camaraderie
Bilis had in his company   1952
two dwarf kings; each was Bilis's man.
One of these was Glodoalan,
the other Gribalo; and they were
stared at by all in stark wonder.   1956
All three were given every sort
of deference, by all the court,
recognized as the royal beings
they were, and cherished much, as kings   1960
must be; for their degree was great.

Arthur desired to celebrate
this time well and appropriately;
Now, with his people gathered, he   1964
felt a deep joy to see them there;
he had a hundred squires prepare
and bathe—he wished to dub them knights;
each man was given, for these rites,   1968
a silken robe of many hues,
of Alexandrian stuff; could choose
the one he thought distinguished him.
Arms were bestowed, and steeds in trim,   1972
and each a swift and agile beast,
and worth a hundred livres, at least.
   Now when Erec received his bride
and all those rites were sanctified,   1976
her proper name was given out.
This must be done; if it is not,
the woman is not married. Thus
folk learned her name, and how she was   1980
christened in the baptistry.
Now the archbishop of Canterbury
blessed her; the bride's name was Enide.
Thus fittingly they did proceed.   1984
   And when the court was gathered there,
there was no minstrel anywhere,
in all that country, who had some
gift of delight, who did not come   1988
to show his talents in that hall
so full of joy and festival;
some whistled, sang, did leaps and vaults
and magic tricks and somersaults;   1992
pipe, flute, and fiddle made joyful noise
with viol's and hurdy-gurdy's voice
and tuneful twang of organ barrels;

and girls formed rings and danced in carols.   1996
Anything that could well excite
joy or abandon or delight
gave its voice to that lively scene;
they played the drum and tambourine,   2000
bagpipes, panpipes, and reeds and strings,
flageolets, trumpets, for serfs and kings.
Of other pleasures, what to say?
Not one passage was closed that day.   2004
In they came at gate and door,
ragged and splendid, rich and poor.
King Arthur was not miserly;
all could eat all they wanted, free.   2008
Pantrymen, butlers, cooks had spread
abundance of meat and wine and bread;
there was no need, no whim, no taste
that would not on that day be graced.   2012
    I could go on and tell you much
of feasting, stuffing, wining, and such;
another pleasure's now in store,
one that has infinitely more   2016
significance. Now listen, hear
of the joys of the bedchamber.
    You shall not hear a tale of dark
dread, in which the lordly Mark   2020
is cheated, and his bride filched away;
no substituted Brangein lay
in hallowed sheets; attending were
bishops, archbishops, to bless the pair.   2024
The queen herself dressed them, and she led
the couple to their waiting bed,
since both were loved by Guinevere.
    And now my audience, you shall hear   2028
of sanctioned bliss: the hunted stag,

panting with thirst on rock and crag;
the hunting falcon, flying home
famished, when summoned, does not come 2032
with more love to the longed-for place
than these two to their first embrace.
Delay had chafed them; but no more,
and some things are worth waiting for. 2036
Now the well-wishers leave the room;
the lovers give each part, each form,
its due. The eyes, first; they express
a special, sweet voluptuousness, 2040
borne to the heart and to each sense.
The more they look, the more intense
their longing grows; soon after this
—and better—they begin to kiss; 2044
kissing makes longing great, makes love
—the drink tasted together—move
their hearts. They drink more rapturously,
a brief pause gives them agony; 2048
with kissing, then, the games begin.
When love is perfect, it can win
the place that was possessed by fear;
there was enough perfection here 2052
to make the girl brave, and she could
allow her lover all he would;
and when she rose, the girl was gone,
and a new woman had been born. 2056
    Jongleurs and players, the next day
rejoiced, for they got ample pay;
all that was due to them they got,
and there were splendid gifts passed out. 2060
Robes of ermine or rabbit fur,
squirrel, or fine cloth with miniver;
silks, or violet stuffs; some chose

horses or coin, and they got those.   2064
Each had whatever suited him,
whatever wish he had, or whim.
For fifteen days there was at court
festivity and joy and sport   2068
and splendor and magnificence.
For joy and royal elegance,
to honor Erec once again,
Arthur had all the lords remain   2072
for a full fortnight; all must stay.
When the third week was on its way,
they all agreed on an event;
they undertook a tournament   2076
between Erec and Tenebroc
and Melic and Meliadoc;
Gawain stepped forth, and it was he
who, on one side, made surety.   2080
Thus was the challenge, the *défi;*
and they all parted severally.

ONE MONTH, THEN, after Pentecost,
they met for tourney and for joust   2084
beneath Tenebroc on the plain.
And there was many a banner seen,
of crimson; many a veil or sleeve,
blue, white, that someone thought to give   2088
as a bright token of their love;
many the lances borne above
the riders; azure, red, these were,
with gold and silver in great store,   2092
and many other ornaments

and bands, and brilliant mingled tints.
Those who were well and smartly placed
saw many iron, steel helmets laced —   2096
green ones, yellow ones, vermilion;
they sparkled like the very sun.
White hauberks, bucklers, rank on rank,
and many swords at the left flank,   2100
so many brilliant shields, fresh, new,
of finest red or azure, blue;
gold buckles on a silver shield.
And oh, the horses in that field!   2104
White-foot, white, sorrel, black, brown, bay,
they rushed together speedily.
    Arms fill the field, conceal its floor,
and from the ranks is raised a roar,   2108
the melee and the fracas rise,
the lances grind with a great noise,
they snap; shields splinter, tearing by,
and hauberks fail and rivets fly,   2112
saddles are emptied, men fall down,
and horses sweat and shine with foam.
Drawing their swords, the warriors rush
on those who've fallen with a crash;   2116
they rush for ransom and reward,
or to save honor with a sword.
Erec rides out on his white mount,
alone, just to the battlefront,   2120
to joust, if he can find a man.
Against him now — it seems he can —
spurs Orguelleus de la Lande,
upon a horse from Ireland,   2124
speeding most smartly down the field.
Upon his chest, upon his shield,

Erec delivers with such force
the proud one's knocked right off his horse;   2128
he leaves the fray and disappears.
Now the knight Randuraz appears;
son to the Dame of Tergalo,
in sendal swathed, from head to toe,   2132
a chevalier of great prowess;
and each to each makes his address.
Now blow on blow each fighter wields,
on necks and shoulders and on shields,   2136
and Erec hurls his lance, to wound
his man and stretch him on the ground.
　　Then Erec found, on his return,
the king of the Red City, one   2140
most valiant, skillful, and adroit.
They take the rein knots now, each knight;
each grasps his buckler by its thong;
each one has weapons fine and strong,   2144
good horses, swift and full of fight.
Under their shields, both new and bright,
with such great force they hurl, they try
their lances, that the splinters fly;   2148
never was witnessed one such blow.
Their shields clash in this rendezvous,
arms, horses, meet; and neither rein,
breast strap, nor cinch can now restrain   2152
the king—they give way, straps and girth,
and he lies stretched upon the earth,
and both the reins and bridle band
he carries with him in his hand;   2156
and all who see this joust now say
—marveling much, with much dismay—
it costs a man too dear a cost

to take this knight up on a joust.   2160
Erec had now no wish or need
to take this chevalier or steed,
but joust, acquit himself, and here
show how his prowess could appear.   2164
Around him rose the battle roar;
his feats, his prowess, urged the more
those all about him in the fray;
he took steeds, knights, in the melee,   2168
his foes' discomfort to obtain.
　　Now I must speak of Sir Gawain,
who so adroitly fought, so well,
and conquered in that fight Guincel   2172
and Gaudin of the Mountain; there
took many a knight and destrier.
Well he performed then, Sir Gawain,
and Gilflez, Do's son, and Yvain,   2176
and Sagremors le Dezreez.
So strong a force they were, such threats,
back to the gates they pushed their foes,
beating, unhorsing most of those.   2180
And now before the castle gate
the two lines rushed; the clash was great,
and those within fought those outside.
Sagremors, thrown down on this ride,   2184
now fell; most worthy chevalier,
he was detained, held captive here,
and to his rescue Erec rushed.
One knight got Erec's lance untrussed;   2188
beneath his breast Erec, with force,
struck, so the man lost seat and horse.
He drew his sword, he thrust, he hit,
and the knights' helmets crushed and split;   2192

they fled, they left the meadow clear,
the boldest of them full of fear.
Hard blows and bold strokes by the score
he gave, to rescue Sagremors,   2196
and drove his foes, in disarray.
    Now vespers sounded. All that day
Erec had met so well the test
that in the melee he was best,   2200
but on the next day he excelled
even himself, and he compelled
thus, many knights, and made them leave
their saddles, fall; none could believe   2204
his skill who had not seen this sight.
On both sides all said of our knight
he'd won the tourney and the field.
His lance was victor, and his shield.   2208
Erec had earned now such renown,
he was the talk, and he alone,
of everyone: he had the grace
of Absalom, he had that face;   2212
the tongue of Solomon, the wit;
a lion's courage, every whit.
His gifts and spending were a wonder,
so that he seemed great Alexander.   2216
    The trials and the tourney done,
Erec now asked his king a boon;
he asked a favor at his hand:
he wished to leave for his own land.   2220
But first he was at pains to thank
his sovereign; courteous and frank
and wise he was; much thanks were due
for all his honors, this he knew.   2224
But now he asked his king for leave;
he wished to journey, wished to leave

and lead his wife to his country.
This boon the king would not deny,　　　2228
though it was not what he liked best.
He granted Erec his request
but begged him, soon, to come again.
Of all his barons, all his men,　　　2232
none was more valiant, skilled, humane,
save his dear nephew, Sir Gawain—
with him none other could compare.
After him Arthur had most care　　　2236
for Erec, prized him, held him dear,
most so of any chevalier.

Erec wished not to linger there,
and now he bade his wife prepare,　　　2240
since they had leave to go from court.
For company and for escort
they'd sixty much-praised chevaliers,
steeds, and furs—vairs and minivers.　　　2244
All was prepared and underway,
and Erec wished not to delay;
now he seeks leave of Guinevere,
commends to God each chevalier.　　　2248
Then the queen gives him leave to part.
Prime sounded; now he made his start,
and he set out from Arthur's hall,
mounting his horse before them all;　　　2252
she mounted after him, his bride.
Thus to his country they would ride.
Now mounted all his entourage,
seven score in that menage,　　　2256
the sergeants and the chevaliers.

NOW THEY PASSED hills, cliffs, rocky tiers,
and forests, mountains, plains, they passed;
they rode four days, and then at last   2260
they came to Carnant, where the king,
the royal Lac, was sojourning.
What a delightful town was there!
No setting could be lovelier.   2264
Forests and fields—these had great charms;
and there were vineyards, there were farms,
rivers and orchards, bright fruit trees,
and chevaliers and fair ladies,   2268
and squires adroit and vigorous,
and clerks well-bred and courteous,
who spent their stipends generously,
and women of nobility   2272
and beauty; burghers prosperous;
castle and town were peopled thus.
    Soon as the castle was in view
Erec sent forth his envoys, two,   2276
who rode ahead of him to bring
news of his coming to the king.
Hearing, the king had mount and ride
clerks, chevaliers, young girls beside;   2280
the horns must sound, and tapestries
be hung for the festivities,
flags flung, of silk, in streets and ways,
to greet his son with joy and praise.   2284
    And now Erec himself has mounted
—fourscore, the clerks that can be counted—
fine men, distinguishing their orders,
in gray fur cloaks with sable borders;   2288
and then five hundred chevaliers
on bay and sorrel destriers;

ladies; bourgeois; a crowd withal.
Who is the man can count them all?   2292
   They gallop now, they run; they see,
they know each other finally,
the king his son and his son he.
Both stand on earth, and joyfully   2296
they kiss each other and embrace.
They stand for some while in that place,
neither man moving from the spot,
holding each other where they've met.   2300
Now the King Lac rejoices so!
At length he lets the young prince go,
turns toward Enide; with ravished senses
gazes at both, the prince and princess,   2304
fall on their necks and kisses them,
not knowing which most pleases him.
   And now within the castle wall
they come; and for their coming, all   2308
the bells ring out their joyful sound;
reeds, wild mint, iris, on the ground
lie strewn beneath the people's feet.
And there are hung in every street   2312
bright weavings and embroideries,
and light silks ripple in the breeze.
What joy in these festivities!
They come, these folk, of all degrees,   2316
to look upon their new seignior;
never has anyone seen more
of joy, in young, or old and gray.
   To the old church they made their way, 2320
and a devout procession here
received the dame and chevalier;
before the crucifix at once

Erec now made his orisons. 2324
And sixty silver marks he gave
—what better purpose could they have?—
also a cross of gold, so fine
made in the reign of Constantine; 2328
in it a piece of the True Cross
on which Our Lord redeemed our loss,
was crucified, was tortured thus,
and from that prison rescued us 2332
which we had so long languished in,
ever since Adam fell to sin
by counsel of our Enemy.
This cross had great worth, plain to see. 2336
Studded it was with precious stones,
of great worth, rich and splendid ones.
At each extremity was placed
a carbuncle, with gold all chased, 2340
a marvel, set so beautifully,
its like you could not hope to see.
Each of these gems shone with such light
it seemed to make a day of night, 2344
like morning when the sun appears.
Their radiance through the dark would pierce
and light the church; one needed here
no candle, lamp, or chandelier. 2348
　　Before Our Lady's altar, then,
Enide came with two noblemen,
to Jesus and the Virgin made
devotions properly, and prayed 2352
that in their lifetimes she would bear
one to reign afterward, an heir.
She offered then a cloth of green,
silk stuff; its like was never seen. 2356

A chasuble, all worked and woven
with finest gold, was also given.
It is proved truth, it is well known,
Morgan la Fée had worked and sewn   2360
this cloth, in the Vale Perilous.
Great art she used to weave it thus.
Of gold and silk of Aumarie
this cloth, and Morgan's artistry.   2364
Not for a chasuble, to chant
the holy service, did she want
this work; she meant this splendid gold
her lover's body to enfold,   2368
she herself was so fey, so fair.
By her own arts, Queen Guinevere,
the mighty Arthur's consort, saw
that through the emperor Gassa   2372
this cloth she'd have. And when she did,
of it a chasuble was made.
In her own chapel long it lay,
so rich it was, of such beauty.   2376
When Enide left the court, the queen
gave it to her, to be her own;
a hundred silver marks, in truth,
or more, this golden silk was worth.   2380
    Making her offering, Enide
now stepped back, crossed herself—a deed
a well-bred lady does. They go
from church to hostel, straight; they show   2384
such joy, such happiness display!
Erec has many gifts that day,
from chevaliers and bourgeoisie.
A palfrey from the north country   2388
is first, and then a golden cup.

This man a golden bird brings up,
a *brachet* or a *lévrier*,
trained to hunt down the fleeting hare;   2392
that one a Spanish destrier.
A sparrow hawk's another's share.
One brings a shield, and one a helm,
a sword, an ensign; in no realm   2396
has ever king been greeted so,
so joyfully and with such show.
They take great pains to serve their prince.
Even more joy, more diligence,   2400
they show Enide; they see in her
beauty that is beyond compare,
kind openness, and noble wit.
    So in a room we see her sit,   2404
on couch, or cushion, coverlet,
of silk from Thessaly; there, met
about her, many lovely wights.
But as a brilliant gem ignites,   2408
and tawny pebbles, while it glows,
seem duller; or the radiant rose
puts bright-hot poppies into shade;
So Enide, in her beauty, made   2412
all maidens, ladies, seem less fair.
Search the world; search out everywhere,
walk the circumference of the earth;
there's been no woman of her worth,   2416
gentle and reasonable, kind,
well-spoken, wise. You could not find
one so disarming, debonair,
open—but full of savoir faire.   2420
Unknown, such quiet sagacity;
no foolishness you'd ever see,

meanness, or nastiness, or spite.
Truly her instincts were for right;   2424
truly well-bred, she'd qualities,
perceptions, generosities,
unmatched; all loved her candid ease.
Who did her service, was most pleased.   2428
No realm, no empire anywhere
knew such a dame, so debonair;
no dame had lovelier ways than she!

BUT EREC LOVED so ardently,   2432
he burned no longer for events
of knightly valor, tournaments;
he showed indifference to them all
and lived, absorbed and sensual,   2436
making her pet and paramour,
still serving and attending her,
kissing, embracing, dallying,
seeking her ease in everything.   2440
    Now grief among his comrades spread;
often among themselves they said
he loved too well, he was not wise.
Often past noon he would arise,   2444
and would not leave her side till then,
happy—though others felt chagrin—
rarely, if ever, far from her.
His ways did not at all deter   2448
his care for knights and followers—
arms, clothes, and coin for chevaliers;
and there was not a tournament
where his own men had not been sent   2452

beautifully, richly, fitted out.
Destriers, chargers, without doubt
fresh for the tourney and the joust,
he gave without regard for cost.   2456
The knights deplored his injured name,
the loss, the grief, the waste, the shame,
that such a man should have no care
for arms and for a knight's career.   2460
    So much remark there was, and blame,
by knights and sergeants, Enide came
to hear of it. She heard them speak,
placing him now among the weak,   2464
feeble at arms and chivalry;
how changed he was, how sad to see!
This talk disturbed, bore down on her.
She hid her thoughts; she did not dare   2468
to tell her lord how matters stood,
so much she feared his bitter mood.
So she concealed the whole affair
until one morning, when the pair   2472
lay close together. Earlier they
had had great pleasure in their play;
now in each others' arms they lay,
still their lips touched, as was their way.   2476
    He was asleep, and she awake;
and now her thoughts began to take
familiar shapes: what most now said
about her lord, the life he led.   2480
So she recalled her thoughts and fears,
and she could not keep back her tears,
weighed down, grief-stricken as she was.
Mischance, which always waits for us,   2484
now made her speak, caught her off guard,

and in her pain she spoke a word
she'd later think showed addled wit.
Just now she saw no harm in it.　　　2488
She looked at him from head to foot,
his body so well made, she thought,
his fine, clear features. Vehemently
she wept. The tears fell fast and free,　　　2492
down on his chest. And as they ran,
"Alas!" she said, "what harm I've done!
Far from my home, what have I found!
Best I'd been buried in the ground.　　　2496
Instead, the best of chevaliers,
hardiest, bravest, and most fierce,
more loyal and more courteous
than counts or kings, the best of us,　　　2500
has fallen, fallen utterly
—for my sake—from all chivalry.
My fault, my shame, this wreck I see!
Oh, that such blame were not for me!　　　2504
Friend, how wretchedly done!" said she.
Then she looked at him silently.
But he was half asleep; he heard
her voice, the sound of it. He stirred,　　　2508
sensing the last words that she spoke.
He surfaced from his sleep, and woke
aghast; she still wept strenuously.
"Friend!" he said. "Sweetheart! Say to me,　　　2512
why do you weep in this dreadful way?
What has injured you so? Please, say.
I will know. I want to know. I must.
Sweet friend, don't hide it; speak in trust.　　　2516
What is it that's done wretchedly?
I know these words referred to me,

not someone else; I have no doubt.
Tell me, what is this all about?   2520
I heard you speak. You have to say."
      She felt great fear then, and dismay,
desperation; she felt them grow.
"Fair sire," she said, "I do not know   2524
what this is that you say to me."
"Lady, just why this secrecy?
Don't hide from me. What can you gain?
You have been crying, that is plain.   2528
This is not something trivial.
Also, I heard you now, heard all
you said. You must explain to me."
"Ah, fair sire, it was possibly   2532
a dream; it must have been, indeed,
if you heard anything." "Enide,
what are these lies you'd serve to me?
Plainly you're lying; obviously.   2536
Admit it now; come now, confess,
or you will add to your distress."
      "Sire," she said, "since you press me so,
I will tell you what truth I know;   2540
I speak with sorrow and with dread.
In this whole country it is said
by all—the fair, the dark, the red—
what shame it is that since you've wed,   2544
you neglect arms and exploits. Oh,
how your great worth has fallen low!
It was long custom, in the speech
of knights together, each to each,   2548
to say none like you could be found,
better and braver, more renowned,
in the whole world. Now they laugh, all—

young folk and white-haired, short and tall, 2552
they call you passé, cowardly!
Can you believe the pain, for me,
to hear them laugh and jeer and mock?
How much it hurts me when they talk. 2556
But what is most unbearable
is that they blame me, fault me, all
accuse me. This is, you see, their view:
I have ensnared and captured you. 2560
They give this reason, every one.
Your worth, your reputation's gone!
And no man finds you venturesome.
Now you must search your mind, find some 2564
way to obliterate this stain
and have your honor back again.
Much blame, too often, I have heard.
I've never dared to speak a word, 2568
but wept, wept with anxiety!
Just now it all swept over me.
I could not help it. Thus, you see,
I said it was done wretchedly." 2572
    "Lady," he said, "you are right. I see.
And they are right, who thus blame me.
Get up. Put on your clothes, prepare
to ride, and get your richest wear. 2576
Get out of bed right now, get dressed;
put on the very loveliest
gown you own, and without delay
have the saddle brought straightaway 2580
for your best palfrey." She obeyed.
    Now she was very much afraid:
she got up, sad and full of thought,
more and more struggling and distraught 2584

at all her folly, all she'd said.
Now she had truly made her bed
and must lie there. "Ah, wicked fool!
foolishly wicked, stupid, cruel   2588
thing that I am! My cup was full,
ran over. Irresponsible,
ungrateful woman, how could I
speak such insensitivity?   2592
God! Did I think his love so poor,
so slight? Too much he loved, that's sure.
I shall be exiled now. The pain,
never to see my lord again—   2596
that will be worst. No one but he
could have such ways, such courtesy!
This was the best knight ever born.
Then he loved me; I saw him turn   2600
away from all else for my love.
All that I wanted I could have.
Oh, I was truly fortunate!
Pride puffed me up to such a state   2604
that I could trespass thus, could be
so wrong, and shamed so rightfully.
Justice I have; fit punishment."
    So she continued to torment   2608
herself, distracted, while she dressed
well and adroitly, in the best
garment of all that she possessed,
wretched, though at her loveliest.   2612
Shame it all seemed now, mockery.
She sends a maid now, hastily,
and summons one of her own squires
and tells him that she now requires   2616
he saddle up her splendid mount,

her Norway palfrey; king or count
could have no better animal.
He does not waste his time at all,   2620
but saddles up her dappled horse.
    Erec has summoned, too, of course,
another squire; he has this man
bring out his arms, has them put on.   2624
He mounts now to a gallery,
has a fine Limoges tapestry
spread out before him on the floor;
and the squire runs now, quickly, for   2628
the arms Erec commands be brought,
and on the rug he lays them out.
At one end of this tapestry
he sits, placed just where one can see   2632
a figured leopard seem to prance.
Now he turns to his arms at once:
laces his greaves up firm and tight,
fine ones of linked mail, steel, all white.   2636
The hauberk, next; so fine, I say,
no one could tear a link away,
so excellent, you must believe,
on right or wrong side of the weave   2640
no trace of iron you'd find therein—
no, not enough to make a pin.
For rust to grow there's not enough;
of silver, triple-wove, this stuff,   2644
with tiny links of mail, and made
so subtly, it can well be said
that he who put the hauberk on
would feel as little grief and pain   2648
as silken tunics chafe or hurt
if slipped on just above a shirt.

Sergeants and chevaliers, they all
marvel to think what will befall: 2652
Why this armed venture? Why this task?
No one, however, dares to ask.
　　He wore the silver hauberk now;
they placed a helmet on his brow,   2656
banded with gold and gems, and bright
as ice that glistens in the light.
A vassal laced it on his head,
belted his sword; and Erec said   2660
his Gascon bay must now be brought,
saddled, prepared. One man he sought:
"Vassal," he said, "run, now, make haste.
Go find the chamber that is placed   2664
just by the tower. Find my wife, say
I'm much annoyed by her delay.
Why does she take so long to dress?
Let her mount, ride; her tardiness   2668
upsets me as I wait." He went,
this vassal, where he had been sent;
he found her dressed, but wild, distraught,
weeping at all her words had wrought.   2672
"Lady," he said, "why dally so?
My lord awaits you here below,
ready to ride some time ago,
armed in his armor. Why so slow?   2676
Why do you tarry in your dress?"
　　Much wonder, then, and much distress,
she felt, and marveled at what plan
her lord had set his mind upon;   2680
but she was wise, and joined him now,
pretended cheer upon her brow.
She joined him in the courtyard square

and the King Lac ran after her.   2684
Vying, hurrying, came the knights,
young men and white-haired, ancient wights,
wanting and seeking, each, to know,
could they ride with him? Could they go?   2688
So each proposes his affairs.
Erec is firm with them; he swears
that of companions he'll have none,
only his wife, and she alone.   2692
Thus he declares; alone he'll be.
    Great is the king's anxiety.
"Fair son, dear son, where will you fare?
Tell me. You must. What's this affair?   2696
Don't hide it from me. Speak, declare
your destination! Tell me where,
since you will not, for all I say,
have in your escort on the way   2700
squire to assist you, friend, or knight.
If now you undertake to fight
in single combat with some man,
you must arrange your needs and plan   2704
at least some escort; then there'll be
for cheer and for good company
chevaliers, some of your own.
A prince does not go forth alone.   2708
Fair son, pack up your horses; make
a traveling band of knights, and take
thirty or forty, even more.
Take gold and silver; take a store   2712
fit for a noble. Do, my son."
    Erec replies, when he has done,
and tells him all, contrives to say
in detail how he'll make his way.   2716

"Sire," he declares, "it cannot be
that I'll lead destriers with me,
or carry silver coins, or gold,
ride with my squires, or sergeants bold;   2720
no company I'll have with me
save for my wife—yes, only she.
I beg: however fate may turn,
if I should die and she return,   2724
then love my wife and hold her dear,
for love of me. Heed, sire, this prayer:
half of your land must go to her,
this without battle, without war,   2728
hers for her lifetime, as her own."
The old king hears; he says, "Fair son,
I promise this, though fear at heart
I feel, to see you thus depart,   2732
alone; great anguish and great woe.
Against my wishes you will go."
"Sire, it can be no other way.
To God I commend you; and I pray,   2736
keep my companions well in mind,
horses and arms, things of the kind
fitting these noble chevaliers."
     The king cannot keep back his tears,   2740
watching his son intent to leave;
the folk around him weep. They grieve,
the ladies and the chevaliers;
they too feel sorrow, and great fears.   2744
Not one but suffers; several
faint where they stand, they reel and fall.
Weeping, they kiss, embrace him; few
are not distraught, wild, through and through.   2748
If he'd his death wound, I believe,
they would not sorrow more, or grieve.

He comforts them; he pleads good sense.
"Why weep with so much vehemence,   2752
my lords? I have no wounds, no pain;
what will this grief and anguish gain?
If now I leave, I will return
when God is pleased, and when I can.   2756
You I commend, now, as I leave,
to God—if you will give me leave.
All of you cause me much delay,
and much depression and dismay,   2760
weeping and carrying on this way."
He commends them to God, and they
commending him, watch him in pain.
He departs now, his wife in train,   2764
for *avanture;* he knows not where.

ℰℬℵ

"COME, NOW," HE says. "Ride fast. Take care
not to presume, and do not dare
to speak. I do not want to hear   2768
of anything along the way.
Hold off from any speech, I say,
until I've spoken first to you.
Now, ride. Ride swiftly. All you do,   2772
do with assurance and with speed."
"As you wish, Sire," replies Enide.
And so she rides, before her lord;
neither to other speaks a word.   2776
    She, desolate, and mourning much,
murmurs again the same reproach,
softly, just to herself, and low.
"Alas!" she says, "I came to know   2780
such joy, God raised me to such bliss!

How soon I was reduced to this!
Fortune, who seemed to beckon me,
withdrew her hand all suddenly.   2784
I'd put in her no stock or store
if I dared speak to my seignior.
Abandonment and death my fate,
he has conceived for me such hate.   2788
For hate it is, well I can see;
he will not even speak to me.
I am not bold; I can't defy
his wishes, nor his hate; not I!"   2792
Thus she debated as she rode.
    A gentleman, now, of the road,
"chevalier of the woods"—in brief,
he made his living as a thief—   2796
lurked there, with two knights' company;
armed to the teeth they were, these three.
Their chief much coveted the steed
—the palfrey—ridden by Enide.   2800
"Men, what awaits you! Do you see?"
he told them. "Lordings, we must be
men of the hour, or live in shame,
cowards, unlucky fools, to blame.   2804
Here comes a lady, beautiful—
I know not whether demoiselle
or married woman, but—what things!
Her palfrey, saddle, breast strap, reins,   2808
all of this harness, and the beast
worth twenty silver marks, at least.
I want the palfrey; you can claim
whatever else you care to name.   2812
I'll have no other for my share.
As God's my witness, friends, I'll swear

that knight shall not lead her away.
I'll be the one to make *défi;*   2816
I promise you, that chevalier
will find his payments very dear.
It's right that I should go and make
the challenge; then we'll win our stake." 2820
The two obliged him; straightaway
he rode to his intended play.
They backed off, hiding in the wood.
By custom it is understood   2824
two knights attack no man alone,
for it must seem that only one
assails the man who is attacked;
else this would seem a cowardly act. 2828
 Now Enide saw these chevaliers;
gripped, she was, shaken, by her tears.
"Ah, God," she said, "what can I say?
They'll kill or seize him, certainly, 2832
for he is one and they are three.
There's no chance, no equality
in such a game; they're three, he's one.
Now, instantly, I see him come,   2836
their leader, taking us off guard.
God! Coward! Not to warn my lord,
can I be such a person? No,
I shall not; I shall speak; he'll know, 2840
I shall not let this matter be."
 She turned to him immediately
and spoke: "Fair sire, think, what to do?
Here come three men, hot after you, 2844
spurring in haste as if to hunt;
vicious, I fear, in their intent."
"What?" said Erec. "You speak? I see,

too well, how much you care for me.   2848
Now with great boldness you speak out,
and callously ignore and flout
the prohibitions I have made.
I will forgive what you have said   2852
this time; but if again you speak,
there'll be no pardon left to seek!"
    He turns, then, with his shield and lance,
toward his assailant makes advance.   2856
The other sees him; makes a shout,
and Erec hears and he calls out
defiance: now they spur and meet,
thrust their long lances in the heat   2860
of quarrel; but then the other fails,
misses, and Erec now assails
the brigand, knowing the right stance,
and gives a great thrust to his lance   2864
that halves the shield; it falls in two,
the hauberk fails; it's bitten through,
snapped, broken up in the knight's chest.
The lance is buried in the breast   2868
straight through the heart, a foot or more.
The point turns in the body's core,
and the man falls. Now die he must,
his heart's blood drunk, the death spear thrust.   2872
Another thief now takes the field,
leaving his fellow still concealed.
He moves with menace toward Erec,
who takes the shield slung round his neck,   2876
holds it, attacks, all hardiness.
The thief rides, shield held at his breast.
They lunge, both, at the shields; they hit,
and now the other's lance is split   2880

and, shattering, it flies apart.
Now straight into the robber's heart
Erec's lance flies, one-fourth its length;
today the other's spread his strength, 2884
he faints and lies upon his back.
And Erec rides to the attack
of the third man; the third one sees,
and, without fuss or bother, flees, 2888
so terrified, he runs away,
seeking some other hideaway.
It does him little good, this flight,
for now Erec pursues the knight. 2892
 "Vassal! Vassal! Turn and fight!
Defend yourself with all your might,
or I'll attack as you turn tail!
You'll find your flight of no avail!" 2896
The other did not care to heed,
but hurried off; he made good speed,
but Erec overtook his foe
and gave his painted shield a blow, 2900
just on the right, that knocked him flat.
So much for those three; that was that,
one killed, one wounded, and, perforce,
the other knocked right off his horse. 2904
Now he must make his way on foot.
Then all three horses Erec put
together, tied their harness, too;
these horses differed much in hue 2908
The first as any milk was white,
the second black—and no mean sight—
the third all dappled gray, or vair.
 Back to the road he must repair 2912
to where Enide waits now, at hand.

And then he gives her his command:
she is to drive these horses three.
Harshly he spoke, and threateningly —   2916
she neither could presume, nor be
bold enough to speak out, but she
must have permission from her lord.
She said, "I'll never speak a word,   2920
fair sire, if you wish that of me."
They went on; she rode silently.

LESS THAN A mile the two had gone.
But in a valley, further on,   2924
five forest knights now saw their chance.
Then in its rest each placed his lance,
all ready; held his shield, all braced,
his shining helmet fastened, laced.   2928
These robbers craved their *avanture.*
They saw the lady; what a lure!
Three destriers she had with her,
and Erec as her follower.   2932
Now when they saw them, with quick speech
they made division, each to each,
of all their trappings and their gear,
as if they'd seized it, free and clear.   2936
It is a wicked thing to covet,
but they had not much profit of it,
for now they met a good defense.
Often one's fooled in these events;   2940
one's object slips and slides away.
Thus it was in this brave assay.
    The first one says that he will try
the lady; her he'll have, or die;   2944

the second says that for his share
he'll claim the dappled destrier;
no more he'll ask, but that fine vair.
The black horse is the third man's care.   2948
"I'll have the white!" the fourth one cries;
the fifth, no coward, his luck tries,
and claims he'll have the destrier
and weapons of the chevalier.   2952
He'll make this conquest on his own;
he'll make the first attack alone,
if all his colleagues will agree;
and they all grant it willingly.   2956
He takes his leave, he rides apace,
his horse is good, and moves with grace.
Now Erec sees him; makes pretense
he's not on guard, makes no defense.   2960
    These forest folk Enide now sees;
blood in her veins stops, seems to freeze.
Terror, dismay, seize her anew.
"Alas," she says, "what shall I do?   2964
I know not what to do or say,
since, if I dare to disobey,
much grief is threatened by my lord
if I should speak to him one word.   2968
But if I don't, he'll die, and what
great comfort will I get from that?
Badly defended, I shall die.
Dear God! He does not sense or spy   2972
these folk; why wait? Poor guilty fool,
chary of words, I've held his rule,
seeking the moment that seemed right;
I see too well, this forest knight   2976
is bent on mischief and on harm.

Dear God! How speak? How give alarm?
He'll kill me. Well, then, I shall die.
I'll not neglect to speak, not I."   2980
   "Sire," she called softly, there in front.
"What!" he replied. "What do you want?"
"Mercy, fair sire! I wish to say,
leaving the thickets by the way,   2984
I've just now seen five chevaliers,
and I can see—I'm full of fears—
they ride against you, to attack;
four of the band are hanging back,   2988
and the fifth rides to this affair
with all the speed his horse can bear.
He'll strike you. Sire, I fear this work.
The others bide their time, they lurk   2992
behind, but hardly far away.
If needed, they will join the fray."
   Erec replied, "Ill is your thought!
You've spoken when I bade you not;   2996
again you've broken my command.
This bears out what I understand,
how small is your regard for me.
You have employed most foolishly   3000
your efforts; I'm not grateful, no;
you have incensed me, that you know.
I've said it—I'll repeat it now—
this time, once more, I'll pardon you.   3004
Next time, control yourself, refrain
from looking round at me again;
do not behave so foolishly.
I will not have you talk to me."   3008
   Against the forest denizen
Erec now spurred; they came, both men,

keen for the fray, they both set to.
The robber's shield from his neck flew,   3012
so hard the blow by Erec thrown;
broken, as well, his collarbone.
His stirrups smashed, he tumbles then;
no fear that he'll get up again,   3016
for many wounds he has, and bruises.
One of his fellows quickly chooses
battle; the two rush to the fray.
No obstacles in Erec's way: 3020
and through the throat, beneath the chin,
the well-forged iron plunges in;
it cuts through bone and nerve to glide
and thrust out through the other side.   3024
The red blood courses down; it rushes
in two streams from the wound, it gushes;
the heart fails, and now flies the ghost.
The third man bounds out from his post   3028
just on the far side of a ford;
into the stream he rushes, toward
Erec, who spurs; and head to head
they thrust, engage, in the stream's bed.   3032
So well does Erec now deliver,
the other man's stretched in the river,
and over him his destrier
falls, drowns the thief, denies him air.   3036
The horse then tries to rise again,
but with much effort and much strain.
    Erec has vanquished, thus, all three;
the other two hold colloquy.   3040
No help for it, they both agree:
they will not stand and fight; they'll flee.
They fly along the riverbanks,

Erec behind, just at their flanks. 3044
He gives one man's spine such a blow
the thief falls on his saddlebow;
so strong the force of his attack
the lance snaps on the robber's back. 3048
He falls, neck first, down on the earth.
Erec now makes him pay full worth
for what his back's done to the lance;
Out comes the sword, to leap and dance. 3052
The man gets up; oh, reckless move!
He takes three blows now from above.
The thirsty sword his blood has drunk;
his shoulder's severed from his trunk, 3056
hewn off, it falls upon the ground.
 And now Erec, who gave this wound,
seeks with his sword, pursues the other,
who's quickly fled in search of cover, 3060
without safe-conduct, route, or plan;
he cannot face or shun his man.
He quits his horse and runs alone,
his faith in it entirely gone; 3064
he throws away his shield and lance
(in them he lacks all confidence),
jumps earthward; Erec does not want
to chase this man who's left his mount, 3068
but stoops; the lance he'll not let lay,
since his was broken in the fray.
He holds the lance; he's armed once more.
The horses, too, he'll not ignore, 3072
but takes all five he wants to lead.
It's hard and painful for Enide,
handling five mounts with the first three.
He orders her to ride; and she 3076

is not to speak to him at all,
lest harm or grief to her befall.
This time Enide does not reply.
Silent she sits; they take their way, 3080
and all eight horses, too, they guide.

❦

TILL NIGHTFALL DID the couple ride;
no inn or town was there to see.
At dusk they took for hostelry 3084
a field, a spot beneath a tree.
Erec commanded the lady
to go to sleep while he stood guard.
Enide refused; she thought it hard, 3088
it was not right; she would not rest.
He should sleep, he'd been harder pressed.
Erec obliged, well pleased to yield;
he laid his head upon his shield, 3092
the lady now her mantle spread,
over his body, feet and head.
    He was asleep, and she awake;
no slumber that night did she take, 3096
but held the horses, watched each one;
all night she held them, till the dawn.
Still she much blamed herself, and still
of her old warning speech spoke ill— 3100
how wrong, how stupid, was her action!
Why, she had not received a fraction
of the distress that she had earned.
"Alas!" she said, "now I have learned 3104
my arrogance; it's been found out.
I know now, without any doubt,

no chevalier is better known
than my own lord, by anyone;   3108
I knew that. Now I learn again;
for right before my eyes I've seen
how with three knights, then five, he came
to fearless strife. Oh, my tongue, shame!   3112
Such shame I spoke in my false pride;
shame in my heart must now abide."
Thus she tore at her soul, all night,
till dawn, and the new morning's light.   3116
    And when the morning light had showed,
Erec got up, and took the road.
She went in front, and he behind.
Now, about noon, the couple find   3120
a squire who rides through a small valley,
And two more young men make their way,
who carry with them bread and wine,
five autumn cheeses, fat and fine.   3124
This squire now hailed them pleasantly.
Seeing the knight and his *amie*
ride through the woods, at once he knew
—shrewd as he was, he could construe—   3128
they'd made some forest glade their inn:
nor had they food or drink therein,
for one could journey for a day
and see no castle on the way,   3132
or town, or tower, or strong-walled keep,
abbey, hostel, or inn, for sleep.
    A kind thought had this squire, and good:
before them in the road he stood,   3136
spoke to them nobly, generously,
and said, "Sire, I suspect—I see—
that you're exhausted and distressed.

Your lady here has had no rest;   3140
your hostel has been this forest.
This white cake here will give you zest,
if you should care to eat a bit.
Come! There're no strings attached to it.   3144
It's of the finest wheat, this cake;
I want no trade for my own sake.
Good wine I've got, too, and fat cheese,
white linens, fine cups; if you please   3148
to lunch awhile, you'll have no need
of further search or further heed.
It's shady here, it has its charms;
divest yourself, sire, of your arms,   3152
come, rest a bit, dismount, sire, do
sit down, as I've invited you."
    Erec stepped to the ground, said he,
"My fair, sweet friend, most willingly   3156
I'll eat, and many thanks to you;
I'll seek no more, but this I'll do."
The squire now well addressed this need,
and from her horse he helped Enide.   3160
The two men with the squire now led
the couple's horses, all eight head.
There they all sat down, in the shade.
And now the squire freed Erec's head   3164
of the bright helm, leaned to unlace
the ventail just before his face;
and then the linen cloth he spread
over the grassy, flowery bed.   3168
The cake he proffered, wine he brought,
and then the cheese prepared and cut;
they who'd been hungry ate their fill,
and drank the wine with great goodwill.   3172

The squire still served them, like a host;
his labor for them was not lost.
They ate and drank; then, for largess
and courtesy, and thoughtfulness,   3176
Erec said, "Friend, a gift I'll make:
one of these horses you must take,
the one that seems best to your sense.
I beg of you—don't take offense—   3180
back to the castle ride, and see
to a fine hostel room for me."
The man responded that he would
find just the room, indeed he could;   3184
he gave the horses a good look,
and chose, with thanks; the black he took.
He thinks it best, the one he wants.
By the left stirrup then he mounts,   3188
and leaves his charges both behind.
And quickly now he rides, to find
a well-appointed lodging house.
Then he returns, and greets them thus: 3192
"Mount up, fair sire, come right away;
I've a fine room where you can stay."
    Now Erec mounts; she follows suit;
the town's close by, just a short route,   3196
and soon they're at their hostelry.
Once there, they're welcomed joyously:
handsomely now the host receives
the two, and all they wish he gives;   3200
with plenty he surrounds the pair,
gaily he does so, with good cheer.
    Now when the squire had done his best,
and in his kindly way addressed   3204
their needs, he took the proffered mount;

before the loggia of the count
he rode the great black animal,
thinking to put him in a stall.   3208
The count saw him approach; he stood
with three liegemen. He turned and said,
"Whose horse is that?" most curious.
"That's your own squire! He's one of us!"   3212
they said. Perplexed and marveling,
the count called down, "This horse you bring,
where did you get him?" "Well, fair sire,
from a great knight!" replied the squire.   3216
"Oh, he was most impressive! Toward
the castle I led him, my lord,
and lodged him at a bourgeois's place.
My lord, such courtesy, such grace,   3220
he has! Such handsomeness! I swear,
on book, on bones, or anywhere,
no man I ever hope to see
has even half of his beauty."   3224
    The count said quickly, "You're naive.
You'll never get me to believe
he's handsomer than I!" "On oath,
you're handsome and well-bred enough,"   3228
his man said. "But there cannot be,
in all the lore of this country
—or of the earth!—a paragon
of beauty like this knight yet born.   3232
I daresay: battered, black and blue,
his hauberk wrecked—still, beside you,
he's patently the better male.
This man could, in the woods, assail   3236
eight knights, all by himself, and lead
away each adversary's steed.

Also, the woman that he's got
is so astonishing there's not　　　　　　　　3240
a single lady anywhere
who's in the smallest thing her peer."
　　When the count heard this latest bit,
an urge to know the truth of it　　　　　　　3244
began to work in him. "*Ma foi!*
Let us go visit this bourgeois.
I never heard such things. Look here,
you must show me this chevalier,　　　　　　3248
you fabricator! Then we'll see
the truth of this hyperbole!"
"Willingly. That's the path. Come on,
it's nearby." And the count came down.　　　3252
"I'd be a fool not to go see,"
he said, descending hastily.
The squire got off the mount, perforce,
then the count climbed up on the horse;　　　3256
the servant hurried to prepare
Erec, and announce his visitor.
　　Erec was resting in the style
he was accustomed to beguile　　　　　　　　3260
his leisure time in. Round the knight
the torches gave a magic light;
many candles, especially
gave the dark air a lambency.　　　　　　　　3264
　　The count assumed a modest air;
he had but three attendants there.
Erec, with manners of a prince,
stood up. "Sire, welcome!" Compliments　　　3268
flowed freely in the atmosphere.
The brave knight and the dapper peer
sat talking on the soft, white bed

and many courteous things were said.   3272
The count was eager to defray
Erec's expenses, or to pay
what Erec owed; elaborately
he begged to do this courtesy.   3276
Our knight denied his needy state,
saying his means were adequate.
They spoke of much; but the count's eyes,
constantly, while he held the guise   3280
of concerned friendship, moved to where
Enide sat, quiet, in her chair.
Her beauty stuns him; more and more
she pleases him; he covets her.   3284
    Now he is seized with amorousness;
and he begins, all charm: "Unless
you, sire, object, I should take leave
for something which, you may believe,   3288
is for your honor. Please, grant me
this delight and this courtesy:
let me sit by your lady. Sire,
I do so very much admire   3292
the two of you. Don't take it ill;
in such a thing I'd have my will.
I wish to serve her, and to do
all that can give her pleasure; you   3296
must see, my dear, perceptive friend,
my love for you inspires this end."
    Erec was not a jealous sort,
and when the count wished to pay court   3300
and please his wife, he saw no harm
or fraudulence, felt no alarm.
"Why should I mind? Do what you please,"
Erec said. "I'm not ill at ease!   3304

Amuse yourself, and speak, and jest!"
So he spoke, and his subtle guest
now moved to purpose and to play.
Now Enide sat not far away,   3308
two lances' distance; her suitor
took a low stool and sat by her.
    Now Enide was both wise and chaste,
with native courtesy and taste.   3312
She turned to him. "Ah, such distress,
lady, I feel, I must confess,
at seeing you so miserable!
It weighs on me and pains me. Still   3316
—believe me!—honor, happiness,
gain, and good things can come from this.
Your beauty will have the rank and state
for which it is appropriate.   3320
You'll be my mistress; and you'll be
mistress, too, of my seigniory—
all that I have and hold, you'll share.
Do not say no to this affair!   3324
I deign, in love, to ask you this.
Your lord does not love you, alas!
or prize you; this I see, I know.
Live with me and be happy so!"   3328
    "Sire," said Enide, "that cannot be.
You waste your time in courting me.
I would that I had not been born,
I'd rather burn in blaze of thorn,   3332
scattered as cinders on the earth,
than compromise my faith, my worth,
to my seignior, who thinks of me
with no idea of treachery!   3336
You are mistaken; there's no chance
exists, with me, for dalliance."

Now rage inflamed the count. "I see.
You are too proud, then, to love me?   3340
No service, suit, or praise, no wit
will bend you to my will, one whit?
Lady, I know so well your sort
of female hypocrite; to court,   3344
pray, beg, flatter; that puffs you up.
Ah, but if made to drink the cup
of bitterness, shamed and traduced—
oh, then you're easily seduced!   3348
You'll not oblige me, hmmm? *Alors,*
I promise you, you will be more
accommodating soon; your knight
and I'll cross swords, and, wrong or right,   3352
I'll kill him, now, before your eyes."
"Sire," said Enide, "take my advice.
This act, uncalled for, treacherous,
—a great sin—will reflect on us.   3356
Now, calm yourself, you know, fair sire,
I will do all that you desire.
Be your brave self; be shrewd; your spoil
is yours for taking; do not spoil   3360
your own intent by hastiness.
It was not pride, sire, I confess
that made me speak! I wished to see
whether you truly, passionately   3364
would love me and would make me yours.
Commit no treason! Nothing's worse!
My lord lacks all suspiciousness;
if you attack and kill him thus,   3368
it will be thought I was the one
who urged you on and wished it done.
All of the land will say this thing
was done by my own counseling—   3372

blood shed, death done, at my behest!
Sire, you must let this matter rest
till morning. When my lord's awake,
then, prudently and quickly, take   3376
advantage, boldly, at one stroke."
Her heart's thoughts were not those she spoke.
    "Now, sire," she said, "have faith in me.
Do not excite yourself, but be   3380
both resolute and shrewd, dear friend.
Tomorrow morning, early, send
your men-at-arms. He will defend
me bravely, but the cherished end   3384
we both desire, you'll reach this way.
Either in joust or in the fray
with many knights, cut off his head.
Oh, what a wretched life I've led,   3388
too long, in such a wretched state!
My lord, I'll not prevaricate:
I'd rather feel your body, pressed
nude to mine, nude in bed, caressed;   3392
be satisfied, my dearest love;
this consummation we'll soon have."
    "Excellent," said the count. "Well said.
Lady, your destiny has made   3396
this fate for you, this gift from me!
I'll treat you well and honorably."
"Sire," she replied, "I know you will.
But plight your troth and promise, still,   3400
you'll treat me well and hold me dear;
or I will have some doubts, I fear."
Joyful, playful, he said to her:
"Take my promise: and I do swear,   3404
loyally as a count, madame,
I will obey your every whim—

or serious wish. Please, have no fears;
I'll have no wants that are not yours."   3408
She took his vow, such as it was,
prizing it little—with good cause.
Yet she was worried, for she had
plighted a promise to this cad.   3412
Her action was, of course, a ruse
to save her lord—a good excuse.
Well, better some mendacity,
and Erec whole—she hoped—and free.   3416
      The count arises, says adieu;
a hundred times he thinks too few.
His joy in this bond will be small.
Erec does not suspect at all,   3420
meanwhile, his death plot by these two.
But God can manage his rescue,
my audience, and I think he will,
though Erec is in great peril,   3424
with no thought of conspiracy
by such a vicious enemy,
who thinks to suddenly dispatch
a wounded man, and then to snatch   3428
his wife and work his pleasure on her;
such is this count's idea of honor.
He takes his leave, with treacherous poise:
"To God I commend you, sire," he says.   3432
"And I you, sire," Erec replies.
Thus they part, with civilities.

MUCH OF THE night had slipped away.
To a room with more privacy   3436
the couple went, found two beds made
upon the floor, and Erec laid

himself on one; the other bed
she took, in anguish and in dread.   3440
No sleep at all she had that night.
How move to action, warn, her knight?
She knew this count, and well she saw
no conscience and no fear of law   3444
could keep the man from his intent;
given his chance to implement
his plan, he surely would not fail
to do it, to the last detail,   3448
and, she was sure, murder with zest.
All night she worried, without rest.
Oh, but if day can bring reprieve,
and she can make Erec believe   3452
his danger, they can flee the place,
the count would waste his time in chase,
not have the lady, nor she him.
    Erec slept long; all night. The dim   3456
new day at last was imminent,
and Enide feared that the moment
of action was delayed too long.
Hers was a loyal love, and strong,   3460
though tender, and her heart was free
from falsehood and duplicity.
She got up quickly now, and dressed,
went to her lord and broke his rest.   3464
"Dear sire, forgive me, but—awake!
Please get up instantly, and make
ready to fly! Conspiracy,
irrational, with no mercy,   3468
is under way; the vicious peer,
the count, will, if he finds you here,
cut off escape and ambush you,

tear you to shreds without ado.　　　　　3472
He's after me; that's why this hate.
God, who knows all, can help our fate,
keep you from capture, or being slain.
Last night the count was all too plain,　　3476
and would have killed you, but for this:
I stopped him with a false promise
to be his lover and his wife.
He's on his way to claim your life,　　　3480
kill you, and then, by force, claim me!"
　　Now Erec saw how loyally
his wife kept faith, under what threat.
"Go down at once," he said, "and get　　3484
our horses saddled. Wake our host,
though at this hour he'll be engrossed
so much in sleep; have him see me.
I've no doubt that this treachery　　　　3488
is well at work, and put to plan."
The saddled horses wait; the man,
wakened, now stumbles from his rest.
Erec has quickly gotten dressed,　　　　3492
and the host come. "Sire, what's this haste?
Why have you now, so grimly, faced
the road at such an hour, before
daylight or sun? What is this for?"　　　3496
　　Erec said he had far to go
and much to do; it must be so,
and added: "Sire, we haven't yet
discussed what payment you should get　　3500
for all the thought and courtesy
that you have shown my wife and me.
These merit much. For my arrears
take seven of my destriers;　　　　　　3504

they do not, by a halter's price
outweigh the worth of your service."
Delighted with his gift, the host
bent double, to his feet, almost,   3508
thanking his guest vociferously.
Erec mounted, then graciously
took leave, and they were on their way.
To Enide he took care to say   3512
firmly, and with much admonition,
that she should make no recognition
of any dangers on the road.
    And now up to the house there rode,   3516
armed to the teeth, a hundred men,
bent on death and destruction. *Tiens,*
the oaths when Erec wasn't found!
The count, whose plans had run aground,   3520
saw, with excoriating wrath,
he'd been led down the garden path.
The marks of horseshoe nails made clear
what it was that had happened here.   3524
Full of rage, and fulminating,
cursing, shouting, and berating,
the count swore he'd have Erec's head.
"Any idiot oaf," he said,   3528
"who lags behind will get hell from me!
But he'll have served me honorably,
that man who can decapitate
this chevalier whom I so hate."   3532
    Headlong they rode into the dust,
blood in their eyes, with murderous lust
for this man whom they'd never seen.
Erec rode; and against the green   3536
line of the woods, along the dim

edge of the woods, they spotted him.
One contender was out in front;
Others deferred, and let him hunt.   3540
Enide now heard the rush and clamor
of all the fighting men in armor
—pounding of horses, clang of arms—
saw the whole valley full, and swarms   3544
of men pursuing; and at that
she could not keep from crying out.
    "Oh, help, sire, help! A host so vast
the count already has amassed   3548
against you, and they're gaining ground!
If you ride to the woods, around
into the thickets, hastily,
we may avoid their company,   3552
since they are still so far behind.
If we continue at this kind
of pace, the price will be severe.
There'll be no equal combat here!"   3556
    "How little," Erec then said, "you prize
me or my words. That you despise
both, is quite clear and plain to me.
How I have wasted time, I see,   3560
in chiding and instructing you!
If God has mercy, and I do
escape, and if my will is yet
not softened toward you, you'll regret   3564
most dearly this disloyalty."
    Now he looks round. Immediately
he sees the seneschal in chase
on a fast horse. There is a space,   3568
still, of four crossbow-shots or so
between them, and this eager foe

has not discarded any gear—
he is well armed. And at his rear   3572
Erec sees a good hundred men;
eyes the chief hunter, who's the one
chasing him hardest, thinks that he
must stop this leading enemy.   3576
Each on his swift and powerful horse,
they come on their collision course,
hurrying, striking, in the field,
trenchant sword upon brilliant shield.   3580
Into his adversary's side
Erec allows his lance to glide
as if the shield and hauberk were
dark blue silk ribbon, nothing more.   3584
       The count spurred onward, furious;
he was, the tale is told to us,
a knight of strength and excellence,
but pride and overconfidence   3588
made him insanely mar his chance.
He carried only spear and lance,
wishing no other weaponry.
And now he rode most hardily   3592
along the field, before his band,
by nine acres, at least, of land.
Erec saw the count plunging on,
and turned toward him. Now neither one   3596
flinched, but they met in frenzied rage;
the count struck first, with such courage
and force, on Erec's breast, the prince
held firmly to his stirrups, since   3600
he'd otherwise have flown. The clang
and crack of Erec's bright shield rang,
loudly, and the count punctured it.

Erec's fine hauberk, so well knit,   3604
delivered him from death that day,
for not a link of mail gave way.
But the count's vigor broke his lance.
And now Erec pursued his chance   3608
ferociously; his steel broke through
his foeman's yellow shield, into
his side, an ell, and now the count
fainted and fell down from his mount.   3612
Then Erec turned and rode away;
his errand done, he did not stay
hanging about, or at his ease,
but swiftly rode on through the trees.   3616
     Now Erec in the forest hid,
and the count's henchmen all stopped dead,
seeing him spread upon the ground;
imprecations and oaths abound.   3620
They swear to hunt the adversary
two or three days, if necessary,
to seize him and to have his head.
And the count heard all that they said.   3624
He stirred himself, and tried to rise
a little bit, opened his eyes;
at last he saw that his pursuit
was bad, and would bring forth bad fruit,   3628
ill conceived, fated for defeat.
He bade his chevaliers retreat.
"My lords," he said, "all, hear me speak.
However bold, or strong, or weak,   3632
or great, or small, you must not dare
to move one step in this affair.
Now, all of you, return at once;
I've acted like a lout, a dunce—   3636

my oafishness, my idiocy!
This lady, though she played with me,
is courteous, brave, intelligent.
I was inflamed to such extent   3640
by her great beauty that I thought
to kill her husband, and then sought
by force to have her; but I see
Fate has now dealt my due to me.   3644
Hypocritical, senseless liar,
I lost all reason in desire!
No mother's ever given birth
to one who'd match this knight's great worth;   3648
try as I would to give him grief,
he was adroit beyond belief
and dealt chagrin instead to me!
And now, my lords, go speedily."   3652
Disconcerted, his vassals all
left, and bore up the seneschal,
and the count, too, stretched on his shield.
Wounded badly, he did not yield   3656
his soul at once, but lived awhile.
And thus Erec survived this trial.

ALL SWIFT INTENT now, Erec rode
between the hedges, down the road.   3660
The woods gave way; before his eyes,
he saw some castle's drawbridge rise
before a donjon of great size.
A wall, a moat, before it lies —   3664
a moat imposing, large, and deep.
Quickly they crossed, approached the keep.

Only a little way they'd come
when on the tower they noticed one   3668
who surely was the sire and lord.
I'll give you now a truthful word
regarding him: the man was small,
but great in heart, and bold withal.   3672
Now he saw Erec on his land.
He hurried down the tower and found
his great, big chestnut destrier,
his saddle with the fine figure   3676
of a gold lion. Now he wants
his shield, his stiff and sturdy lance,
commands his trenchant sword, so bright,
his helmet, glittering in the light,   3680
his fine white hauberk, and each piece
of steel mesh armor. By the *lices*
he's seen a chevalier pass by,
' and now he wants, himself, to try   3684
the man, exhaust him; or, undone,
know he's the weak and recreant one.
Men follow orders, rush about;
see, here, where one of them leads out   3688
the war-horse, brings the saddle, bridle.
And other men are no more idle:
one brings his shield; another man
brings out the arms. Quick as he can   3692
the knight rides out the gate, alone.
Comrades or seconds he'll have none.
    Erec has sought the hill's steep sides;
but, look! the chevalier now rides   3696
at full speed, on a breakneck course,
down a small rise, a wild, mad horse
that snorts and plunges. Its fierce feet

pound at the stones and pebbles, beat   3700
the rocks to meal, as mills grind wheat,
and just as quickly, raising heat
and sparks, clear, glowing ones that soar
in all directions. Now its four   3704
feet, flashing, strike and glow, and seem,
as the horse runs, to throw out flame.
    Enide hears, and is terrified.
Now she can barely keep astride   3708
her palfrey. Sick and faint in mood,
immobilized, she feels the blood
struck still in every vein. Her color
drains and becomes a ghastly pallor,   3712
ghostly indeed, a dead girl's face.
Now despair has her, for her case
is terrible. She cannot dare
to speak a word to her seignior.   3716
Fault is hers either way, and crime;
shall she keep still, or warn in time?
She weighs her thoughts. What's to be done?
She'll speak. And now, her struggling tongue   3720
forms words. Poor girl, her voice is blocked;
her teeth, from fear, have set and locked,
her words are prisoners inside.
Thus her own justice she's applied,   3724
her torture. Now her teeth are clenched;
no word escapes, but all are quenched.
But this, alas, is psychic war!
For now she thinks, "Ah, God! I'm sure   3728
that vicious blame will come to me
if thus I let my seignior die.
Shall I then speak up openly?
God, no! Why not? Oh, he will be   3732

so wild with rage, I do not dare;
if I enrage my dear seignior,
he may just leave me in this spot,
alone, cast off. Oh, then my lot   3736
will be more wretched still by far.
More wretched! God! What do I care?
Never again will I be free
from pain and weight of misery,   3740
while I'm alive, if I don't now,
instantly, help my lord somehow—
help him escape, force out my breath,
or he'll be wounded to the death.   3744
If I don't speak to him at once,
this chevalier will seize his chance,
and have him dead before he's wary.
He seems an evil adversary!   3748
Alas, I've waited far too long;
his speech forbidding me was strong,
but I won't hold back now, for that!
I see so well he's lost in thought,   3752
forgetting all—himself, the knight.
I'll speak. I must. It's only right."
And so she does. He threatens her
again, but he has no desire   3756
to harm her. He knows well enough
that before all she puts her love.
He himself could not love her more.

    He makes his move. He rides before   3760
the chevalier who'd like a fight.
Then at the bridgehead, knight with knight,
they come together, make *défi;*
their iron tips ring out brilliantly,   3764
with all their force each hurls his lance.

Their shields have no more resistance
than bark hung round the neck or back.
The leather rips; planks split and crack;   3768
the hauberks tear, their bright links cut.
Both men are pierced close to the gut.
Each impales each, gives wound for wound;
their horses fall upon the ground.   3772
Neither man gets his death wound yet;
for both have bucklers strong and stout.
    Unhorsed, they throw their lances down
upon the field. Their swords are drawn   3776
swiftly from sheaths. They rush together
in rage; they taunt and goad each other;
neither man means to spare his foe.
The helmets ring from blow on blow,   3780
sparks from the metal flare and dart,
and shields break up and fall apart.
In many places now the swords
have found the flesh beneath its guards;   3784
both men are weak and drained and battered.
If those two swords had never shattered,
but had held up in vigorous play,
neither man would have given way   3788
or quit the fight, while each had breath,
until one fell and found his death.
    Enide was watching. Fear and pain
gripped her, and she was hardly sane.   3792
Anyone there observing her
wringing her hands, tearing her hair,
who watched the tears stream from her eyes,
would, if he had sense, recognize   3796
a loyal lady. He'd have great
pity for one in such a state,
or he'd be some degenerate!

They trade great blows. Now it grows late;   3800
from terce to none they've struggled on,
in such fierce fight that anyone
watching the two could not be sure
which was the better chevalier.   3804
Erec steps up his force and pace;
his sword cuts through the helm, to graze
the chain-mail cap. The other sways
and totters; then regains his grace.   3808
He rushed toward Erec then; so hard
he hit the bright shield with his sword,
the blade wedged in a cleft and stuck,
and when he drew it out, it broke   3812
though a fine sword, and of great price.
Now the knight saw the broken piece,
the remnant of his powerful sword,
held in his hand. He threw the shard   3816
far away, hard as he could throw,
wild with dismay and rage and woe.
Fear gripped him now. He must, perforce,
retreat, since now he had no force   3820
or means to press his cause. What plight
is quite like that of swordless knight?
Erec moves in; the vanquished man
must plead for life as best he can.   3824
    "Mercy, sir noble knight," said he.
"Do not destroy me savagely
because my sword failed in this fight.
You have the force, and legal right,   3828
to kill me, to dispatch me, or
spare me and take me prisoner,
defenseless as I am." "Then say,
when you do thus petition me,   3832
say without reservation that

you have been vanquished in fair fight,
and overcome. I'll raise no hand
again; but be at my command."   3836
      The other paused. Erec, at that
—to give him more to think about—
rushed him again with his short sword.
Dismayed, the other spoke. "My lord,   3840
sire, mercy! You have vanquished me,
yours, without doubt, the victory—
since otherwise it cannot be."
Erec replied, "You must agree   3844
to more; we're not quits yet. Sire, state
to me your name and your estate,
and I will tell you mine as well."
      "Sire," said the other, "you say well.   3848
King I am of this piece of earth;
my liegemen are of Irish birth.
Not one but owes his rent to me.
I am called Guivret le Petit.   3852
Mighty I am; I hold great sway
through all these lands, by every way
each baron and each neighbor lord
does my command, obeys my word.   3856
Not one but does my pleasure; bold,
proud though they be, my neighbors hold
Guivret in dread. Henceforth I want
to be your friend and confidant."   3860
      Erec replies, "I, too, can claim
a gentle birth and noble name.
I am called Erec, and I spring,
the son and scion, from a great king.   3864
He is King Lac of Outer Wales.
And there his sovereignty prevails

over resplendent cities; halls
shining with beauty; mighty walls   3868
of fortresses. All are my sire's;
no kingdoms, no immense empires
have more, save Arthur's lands alone.
Him I except, in truth. No one   3872
is like to Arthur; none's his peer."
    King Guivret wondered much to hear,
and said: "I marvel greatly, sire.
Nothing could make me happier   3876
than your acquaintance, noble prince.
Now you must have full confidence
in me. Perhaps you will remain
here among us, in my domain,   3880
given great honor. You will be
liege lord, in your sojourn, over me.
Both of us need a surgeon. Come,
I have a castle nearby, some   3884
six leagues or seven; not so far.
I wish, fair sire, to lead you there.
There they will tend our wounds for us."
    Erec said, "This is courteous.   3888
I thank you, sire, for all you say.
But pardon me; I will not stay.
I will, my lord, make one request.
If I should find myself hard pressed,   3892
and news should reach you of my need,
then, sire, I would much want your aid.
Think, then, of me, and freely give."
"Fair sire, I swear it. While I live,   3896
if you should find necessity,
ever, to ask for help from me,
I will bring forces to the task,

all I have." "More I cannot ask,"   3900
said Erec. "You have promised much.
You are my lord and friend, if such
words bring forth deeds of equal grace."
    The two knights kiss, then, and embrace.   3904
Never, after so fierce a fray
has there been such a warm display
of friendship shown in parting. See
how, in their generosity   3908
and love, each takes and tears a strip
from his own shirt, and then binds up
the other's hurts, with long, wide bands!
When they had bound each other's wounds,   3912
they said adieu. So it was done;
they parted: Guivret, all alone,
returned, and Erec once again
took up his road and journeyed on,   3916
needing most urgently a salve
or unguent, for his wounds were grave.
He did not stop until he rode
on a plain by a lofty wood.   3920
A forest full of stags and does,
and fallow deer, and fawns, and roes,
and all wild creatures, could be seen.

                          colophon

AND THERE KING Arthur and the queen,   3924
and all their greater barons, lay.
They had arrived that very day,
for the king wished to sojourn there
in this same wood, three days or four,   3928
for play and pleasure, game and sport.

Thus he commanded to have brought
tents and pavilions. To the tent
of Arthur, my lord Gawain went,   3932
worn from a long, exhausting ride;
near the tent door, just by its side,
a birch tree stood. Sir Gawain here
hung up his shield; his ashwood spear   3936
hung by its strap; then Sir Gawain
tied up his horse there by the rein,
saddled and curbed. This animal
was seen by Kay, the seneschal,   3940
who with hot haste had come this way.
And now, in his impetuous way,
Kay thought that, for the joy of it,
he'd take the horse for just a bit.   3944
So up he mounted, did Sir Kay.
No one inquired, or said him nay.
He took the lance, and then made free,
too, with the shield beneath the tree.   3948
Mounted on Gringalet this way,
into a valley rode Sir Kay,
and, as it happened, as he rode
Erec now met him on the road.   3952
   Erec, of course, knew right away
this was the seneschal, Sir Kay,
and, too, he knew the arms, of course,
whose shield it was, and whose the horse.   3956
Kay did not know Erec, because
arms gave no sign of who he was.
So many thrusts of sword and lance
had fallen there, with hammering glance   3960
and battering blows, the paint was gone,
and sign of Erec there was none.

The lady, with her gracious mien,
did not at all wish to be seen   3964
or recognized. She hid her face,
holding her veil up well in place
against the dust and glare of sun—
a tactful ruse. Sir Kay came on,   3968
in great, hot haste; and then by force
he seized the reins of Erec's horse
without saluting him, at once,
and, with his usual arrogance,   3972
before Erec could move or go,
cried, "Who are you? I want to know,
Knight, where you come from. Speak! You must."
     "You must be mad to seize me thus,"   3976
said Erec. "You'll not know today."
"Do not be angry," said Sir Kay.
"For your own good I ask. I see
you have been wounded seriously.   3980
This night, take hostel, sire, with me.
Come, if you wish, and you will be
succored, and treated with great care,
made comfortable and honored there.   3984
Come, sire, you've need of rest. Nearby
King Arthur and his queen now lie
with all their tents, within a wood.
Fair sire, I'll make my promise good: 3988
if you will come along with me,
and see the king and queen, there'll be
great joy made of it—and of you.
And you will have much honor, too."   3992
     "You say well," Erec said. "But no:
not for the world. I will not go.
My needs, and how my mind is set,

you do not know, and I have yet 3996
some way to ride. Sire, let me be.
There is some daylight left to me.
I've delayed much too long." Said Kay:
"This is sheer madness, what you say, 4000
that you refuse to come with me.
You'll regret such stupidity,
for I believe, sir knight—I know—
you and your wife, you both will go, 4004
whether it is your will or no,
just like the priest, compelled to show
up at the synod. Come along;
you'll do yourselves a foolish wrong, 4008
resisting. Come! I'm taking you."
    Fury seized Erec. "What you do,
vassal—or try—is lunacy.
You think to drag me, forcefully, 4012
behind you? You make no *défi*,
just seize me? You've offended me.
I thought my safety was assured,
and did not put myself on guard 4016
against you." Hand upon his sword,
he said: "Now, vassal, by my word,
release my bridle. Step aside!
I know your sort, puffed up with pride, 4020
presumptuous. Drag me after you,
will you? Vassal, if you do,
believe me, I will strike. Away!
Let me alone!" At that, Sir Kay 4024
let go his hold; he turned and wheeled,
more than an acre, down the field,
and then wheeled back, and made *défi*,
like one who means some vicious spree. 4028

They flew at each other. Erec was
noble in fray, and generous;
Kay was unarmed, and Erec thus
turned his lance round, and made his thrust   4032
with butt-end outward. Even so,
he dealt the other man a blow
on his broad shield, so that it struck
his temple. Then his arm was stuck,   4036
pinned to his breast, and Kay fell down,
pushed to the ground, where he lay prone.
Erec now took the horse, to lead
it by the harness to Enide,   4040
and would have led it off, but Kay,
who did know much of flattery,
was now most generous and polite.
Smooth words and fair he gave the knight.   4044
    "Vassal, so help me God, I swear
I do not own this destrier.
That knight who owns him is of worth
and prowess greatest on this earth.   4048
He is my lord Gawain the Bold.
All of this matter I have told
so that you may return the horse;
then, sire, great honor may be yours,   4052
for you'll be wise and generous,
and I will bear your message, thus."
Erec replied, "Then, vassal, pray,
here is the horse; lead him away.   4056
If it's Sir Gawain's destrier,
I have no right or claim, that's sure."
Kay takes the horse. Again he mounts,
rides to the king's tent, and recounts   4060

the truth; he leaves out not a thing.
Gawain is summoned by the king.
   "Fair nephew Gawain"—he spoke thus—
"if you were ever courteous 4064
and noble, do this; instantly
go now, make friendly inquiry.
What's this man's state and business?
Draw him; get him to come to us. 4068
Lead him here with you; do not fail
to do that, if it's possible."
   Gawain mounts Gringalet and goes;
two young squires follow. Erec knows 4072
these squires and Gawain, all, by sight.
They think he is some stranger knight.
Gawain salutes Erec, and he,
likewise, performs this courtesy. 4076
When they've observed it, each to each,
Gawain makes frank and courteous speech.
"Sire," he begins, "I'm sent your way
by the king Arthur, to convey 4080
you to him; king and queen both send
their greeting, and they urge you, friend,
to be their guest here in this wood.
It cannot harm; it may do good. 4084
Sire, come. It is not far from here."
Erec replied, "Fair chevalier,
much thanks to king and queen; and you,
whose courtesy seems wise and true. 4088
I'm weakened, sire; I am not well,
and I have wounds, as you can tell.
But nonetheless, I will not stray
—not for king's lodging—from my way. 4092

Sire, do not waste your time, but leave.
You have my thanks, you may believe."
    Gawain had great good sense. He drew
back now, and made a whispered cue   4096
in one attendant's ear, to go
straight to the king and let him know:
he must give orders and command
the tents be disassembled and   4100
carried three leagues, or four; bestowed,
then, in the middle of the road,
tents of fine linen—have them brought,
said Gawain, nearer this same spot.   4104
"Here must the king lodge," said Gawain,
"if he would meet and entertain
the best knight—I say truthfully—
whom he can ever hope to see,   4108
but who will not, for anyone,
stir from his way. Obliging none,
he will not seek a lodging place."
The man goes off. He speaks his case;   4112
the king must straightaway make sure
the tents are taken down. They are;
the sumpter mules are, in due course,
loaded; the king, on his own horse,   4116
mounts up; and then the queen, besides,
on her own white Norse palfrey rides.
    Now all this while, my lord Gawain
tried, without stopping, to detain   4120
Erec, who said, "Sire, yesterday
I rode much farther; now, today,
I've lost time. You annoy me, sire.
Leave me alone. Your efforts tire   4124
me much; you've much disturbed my day."

Sir Gawain said, "A little way
I wish to go with you, sir knight.
Don't be annoyed. Think; before night   4128
there's still much daylight left to you."
Thus they conversed some time, these two,
until the tents had been spread out.
Erec now saw how he'd been caught.   4132
    "*Haï!*" he said. "Gawain, *haï!*
Your shrewdness has outwitted me,
you've caught me. Such sagacity!
Since you've connived so cleverly,   4136
let me at once give you my name.
Secrecy is no more the game;
I am Erec. In the times past
I was your friend. I am your lost   4140
companion." Gawain hears Erec;
he runs now, falls upon his neck,
hugs the man, and his helmet raises,
and now the ventail he unlaces,   4144
joyous, embraces him again.
Likewise Erec now greets Gawain.
    Now Gawain takes his leave. "I bring
this news, sire, to my lord the king;   4148
he will be overjoyed, both he
and Guinevere, my dear lady.
I'll ride ahead, to speak of it.
But first, let me embrace and greet   4152
Lady Enide, your wife, and give
her loving words, before I leave.
I know my lady Guinevere
has a great longing to see her,   4156
spoke of her only yesterday."
He went up to her straightaway

to ask her how she was, and what
health and what spirits were her lot.   4160
And she responded courteously:
"Grief and pain would be far from me,
if my lord's pain were not severe.
Hardly a limb of his, I fear,   4164
is without wounds and dreadful pain."
"That grieves me greatly," said Gawain.
"Yes, I can see it in his face,
pale as it is, and colorless.   4168
I could have wept just now, alas,
to see how pale and wan he was,
but that my joy was so intense
at seeing him, that all my sense   4172
of his great suffering was effaced.
Now, ride a slow and careful pace;
I will be swift, I will be keen,
and bear this news to king and queen,   4176
and say that you come after me.
I know they'll hear this joyfully."
Saying so much, then Gawain went.
"Sire," he said at King Arthur's tent,   4180
"great joy is ours. I come to say
Erec and Enide ride this way."
For joy the king jumps to his feet.
"This makes my happiness complete,"   4184
he says. "No other news could cause
rejoicing in me as this does."
Quickly he hurries from his tent,
and a crowd rushes with him, bent   4188
on meeting Erec, who can see
the king approaching. Instantly
he jumps to earth; and, too, Enide
slides from the saddle of her steed.   4192

The king falls on their necks. The queen
tenderly kisses them, each one;
and in the crowd the joy runs high.
Each of the knights there has to try   4196
to divest Erec of his gear,
and then they see his wounds. Anger
replaces joy; they all feel rage,
the king and all his entourage.   4200
Now Arthur has an unguent brought,
something his sister Morgan wrought.
This ointment of Morgan la Fée
had such a powerful property   4204
that if applied to any wound
on nerve or joint, the salve was bound,
within a week's time, without fail,
to make the patient whole and hale,   4208
provided that he every day
applied the ointment faithfully.
This salve was brought, then, to the king;
Erec found it most comforting.   4212
    When they had washed and cleaned his wound,
applied the salve, and had it bound,
the king led Erec and Enide
to his own chamber, where he said   4216
that, for his love of them, he would,
for fifteen days, stay in this wood
until Erec was hale and cured.
Then Erec thanked him for this word,   4220
and said, "Fair sire, these wounds you see
are not so difficult for me
to make me pause more on my way.
No one, my liege, could make me stay.   4224
I'll go tomorrow, just as soon
as I can see approaching dawn."

The king attended; raised his head;
"This is a great mistake," he said,   4228
"for you not to remain with us.
I know your wounds are serious.
Stay; it is wisest. For, reflect,
what pity, and what promise wrecked,   4232
your dying in the wilderness
would mean. Oh, dear friend, stay with us,
until you are yourself again."
"Enough, now, sire; this talk is vain.   4236
I have engaged to do this task.
Nothing can make me stay. Don't ask."
    [The king said not another word.
He gave commands to have prepared   4240
the supper; ordered tables placed;
and to the task the servants raced.]
This was Saturday night. First fish,
then fruit, made up the evening dish.   4244
Salmon and perch and pike were theirs,
trout, too; then raw and sweet cooked pears.
After this handsome sustenance,
they had the beds made up at once.   4248
Arthur much loved the wounded man;
he had him laid in bed alone,
where none could touch his wounds. Thus blessed,
he had good lodging and good rest.   4252
Enide and Guinevere, next door,
shared a bed, wrapped in royal fur,
warm ermine; all had good repose
till dawn broke, and the sun arose.   4256
    Erec arises with the dawn,
hastily puts his garments on,
gives commands, has his horse led out

and saddled, and his armor brought. 4260
The squires come running to his need.
Once more the king and knights all plead
and beg Sir Erec to remain.
Their pleas and prayers are all in vain. 4264
He will not pause, for all their fears.
Now you might see them all in tears,
showing as strenuous a dread
and grief, as if they saw him dead. 4268
But Erec arms himself. Enide
gets up. The others mourn and plead,
sure they will never see again
this couple whom they can't detain. 4272
Out from the tents, knights pour, to be
an escort and a company,
and they send quickly for their mounts.
And Erec says, "Take no offense: 4276
you will not ride a step with me.
For all your kindness, gramercy;
I thank you if you all will stay."
His horse is brought. Without delay 4280
he mounts and takes his shield and lance;
commends them all to God at once
and they in turn all say adieu.
Now Enide mounts, and off they go. 4284

THEY FOUND A forest. Now they rode
into the thickness of this wood,
taking no pause or resting time;
they rode until the hour of prime. 4288
Then, at a distance, they could hear

a cry, of terror and despair,
a girl's. Sir Erec heard the noise,
and knew at once it was the voice   4292
of one in pain. He knew that he
must ride and help immediately.
At once he called Enide. He said,
"Madame, some girl goes through this wood   4296
crying and shrieking miserably,
and in my judgment she must be
in need of help. I want to ride
over to her, and offer aid.   4300
Dismount here. Wait here while I go
see what is wrong and what to do."
"Sire," said Enide, "most willingly."
She stayed, and he went off to see   4304
the girl, and give what help he could.
    He found her soon, there in the wood,
weeping and shrieking piteously
for her poor lover, her *ami,*   4308
seized by two giants. Frightful, the way
the ogres led and forced their prey.
The poor girl tore her garments; tore
her tender face, all scratched and sore   4312
and crimson where her nails had grazed.
This Erec saw; he was amazed,
and begged her: what untoward event
had caused such cries, so vehement,   4316
so fierce in their intensity?
She wept, and then she heaved a sigh,
and, sighing thus, she managed: "Sire,
it is no wonder when so dire   4320
a grief is mine. I wish to die.
I do not prize my life. And why,

you ask? My lover has been seized
by his two mortal enemies,   4324
two vicious giants. God on high,
what shall I do? For such as I
—cowardly, paltry—how survive,
when the best chevalier alive   4328
is lost to me? Ah, God, he was
the noblest, the most courteous.
[And now he is in great peril;
This giant pair will surely kill   4332
him, a death most horrible!]
Oh, noble knight, I pray you will,
for God's sake, succor my dear friend,
if that is in your power. Defend   4336
and help us! You need not run far;
close by, close by, they wage their war."
    "Demoiselle, I will go pursue
these giants, as you ask me to;   4340
you may be certain I shall do
all in my power. Either I, too,
will be a captive, or deliver
out of their viciousness, your lover.   4344
If these two oafs have let him live
thus far, I promise, I shall give
what strength I have the power to use,
and summon it to prove your cause."   4348
"Oh, noble chevalier," she says,
"I'll be your servant all my days
if you return my love to me.
I commend you to God's mercy.   4352
Make haste, I beg you, chevalier."
"Which way was it they went?" "Right here.
See, here, the path, the horses' prints."

Erec is galloping at once;   4356
he asks her to await him there.
Again she says adieu. Her prayer
is tender; now she begs the Lord
to grant of His divine accord   4360
strength to Erec, to mortify
those who would her poor love destroy.
    Erec rode off along the course
the girl had shown. He spurred his horse,   4364
chasing the giants. Intent, he rode,
until he saw them in the wood,
not yet come out into the clear.
Stripped of his clothes, the chevalier   4368
rode naked on a nag. As if
he were a common, captured thief,
they'd tied him, hands and feet secured.
They themselves bore no whetted sword,   4372
no shield, no lance; each was equipped
with club and scourge, and each one whipped
the poor stripped man ferociously.
So beaten, bruised, and slashed was he,   4376
the flesh so harrowed from attack,
bone showed in cuts all down his back;
all down his sides and flanks, one wound.
The blood flowed freely to the ground,   4380
so that the nag on which he rode
was, to its belly, soaked in blood.
    Erec, alone, rides after them.
Sorrow and anguish rise in him,   4384
watching the shamed and bleeding knight
suffer such torment and despite.
Now in a meadow, near the trees,
he catches up with them, and cries: 4388

"Seigniors, what wrong has this man done,
that you must beat him to the bone?
What crime deserves this outrage? Why
force on him this atrocity?   4392
Is he a thief? Why, viciously,
drag him? You ogres, did you see
him do some shame, or rob, or steal?
You yourselves act the criminal,   4396
stripping a knight, binding him, nude,
beating him. Shameful act, and lewd!
I ask you, lords; hand him to me,
for fairness' sake; in courtesy.   4400
I do not wish to act with force."
     "What business is it, then, of yours,
vassal? Are you a lunatic,
asking us favors? Well, be quick,   4404
mend matters if they anger you."
"Indeed, they anger me. You two
will not abduct him easily.
Since you have left the choice with me,   4408
let him who can establish right.
I make *défi*. On guard, and fight!
Not one step further on he goes
Till you, too, lords, have tasted blows!"   4412
"Vassal, you must be mad, to thus
try to attempt a quarrel with us.
If you were not one man, but four,
your little strength could do no more   4416
than one lamb that attacks two wolves!"
"Oh? Let us see, then, what Fate proves,"
said Erec. "If the heavens fall,
and the earth melts, then, surely, shall   4420
a lark or two be caught, withal;

some men boast large who turn out small.
Lords, I require you. Stand on guard!"
    Powerful, fierce, his foes fight hard;   4424
fists clenched, they fall to this affair,
clutching their truncheons, huge and square.
Erec rides toward them, lance at rest.
No dread he feels of their menace,   4428
their towering pride. He makes his try,
striking the first one in the eye,
making of blood and brains such wreck,
they spurt out from the ogre's neck,   4432
and he falls dead; his heart has failed.
The other sees him die; now, wild
with anguish—he has cause indeed!—
vengeance propels him in his need.   4436
Club in both hands, he thinks to do
one adroit, devastating coup
on Erec's unprotected crown.
Erec, though, sees the blow come down;   4440
raising his shield, he waits for it,
takes it. It is a vicious hit,
stunning him with such dreadful force,
he nearly falls down off his horse.   4444
But, his shield high, he wards off blows.
Quickly the giant regains his pose,
thinking his second strike will tell,
fall, with full force, on Erec's skull.   4448
    Erec, sword drawn, is ready. Quick,
balanced, assured, he gives attack,
service the giant can't expect;
fiercely he strikes him on the neck,   4452
splitting him to the saddlebow,
scattering his entrails. Now his foe

falls, dead weight, where he cannot rise;
carved into pieces, there he lies.   4456
  Now the poor captive chevalier
weeps in his joy, and thanks in prayer
God, who sent succor in His grace.
Erec proceeds now to unlace   4460
his bonds; puts on him clothes and gear,
mounts him upon a destrier,
asks him to lead the other one.
That done, he asks the rescued man   4464
what is his name, and his estate?
And the man answers, "Noble knight,
you are, by rights, my liege and sire.
Let me fulfill my just desire   4468
and swear homage and faith to you.
You saved my life. Such troth is due;
almost my body and my soul
were hacked apart, in horrible   4472
torment and pain. What *avanture,*
oh, fair, sweet sire, has led you here,
and rescued me, by God's sweet grace?
Out of the hands of enemies   4476
your courage has delivered me.
Homage is due you; fealty,
the loyalty of all my days.
Sire, let this be," the freed man says.   4480
  Erec perceives the keen intent
the other has, how truly meant
the homage he would freely give,
and says: "My friend, I will not have   4484
this service that you offer me.
You must know, it was your *amie*
whose prayers brought me to your relief.

I found her in these woods; in grief   4488
she moaned and shrieked; her pain was great;
truly her heart is desolate.
I must present you to her, then;
when you are joined with her again   4492
I will go on my way alone.
There is no need for you to come;
I have no need of company.
But, sire, please tell your name to me."   4496
    The other said, "With pleasure, sire.
Since you have spoken your desire,
I should not hide my name at all.
[My name's Cadoc de Tabriol,   4500
fair sire; that is the name they call
me by. If it is possible,
tell me your name and country, knight,
since we must part, and then I might   4504
seek you and find you henceforth, when
I leave this land and venture on."
    "Friend, I will never tell you that,"
said Erec. "Speak no more of it.]   4508
If you would truly honor me,
you must go off now, hastily,
without delay, and you must ride
to my liege, Arthur, on this side   4512
of the great woods. He's at the chase,
and, with the vigor of his ways,
looks there for game. I think he's near;
you'll find him five short leagues from here.   4516
Go, go at once, and say to him,
you are a gift, and sent by one
who, in the king's tent, just last night
he entertained with great delight.   4520

And, sire, do not keep secrecy;
tell him how I have set you free
from pain to soul and body too.
I am much loved at court. If you   4524
present yourself there in my name,
you give me honor there, and fame.
There, you may make your inquiries;
you will not know me, otherwise."   4528
"Sire, I will do most speedily,"
said Cadoc, "what you ask of me.
Never take thought, or have a doubt
I go without a willing heart.   4532
I'll tell the whole truth to the king:
the battle, and your succoring."
      Thus, with this talk, they made their way,
returned to where the poor girl lay,   4536
where Erec left her in despair.
Now, what a joyful spirit there,
seeing her lover ride there, plain,
whom she'd not thought to see again.   4540
Erec presents him; takes his hand.
"Demoiselle," says he, "look, I've found
your lover! Leave your grief. Here, see,
whole and rejoicing, your *ami*."   4544
This girl was wise, and courteous.
"Sire," she said, "by right, both of us
are your fair winnings, he and I.
We owe you service. We must try,   4548
as we best can, to honor you.
How can we render what is due?
How pay our debt, by half?" Said he,
"Spare your concern, sweet, fair *amie*.   4552
I ask no guerdon of you two.

To God I commend you both. Adieu.
Too much delay, I think, I've made."
He turned his horse around, that said;   4556
fast as he could, he rode away.
The others rode another way;
the knight, Cadoc of Tabriol,
and his fair girl, his demoiselle,   4560
to king and queen they brought their news.

EREC RODE ON, without a pause;
swiftly he urged, he spurred, his steed,
hurrying back to find Enide.   4564
Grim were the thoughts attending her;
she was persuaded, she was sure
he had abandoned her at last.
Erec, alarmed now, and aghast,   4568
feared she'd been led off, to fulfill
some lecher's hopes, and do his will.
In haste and fear he made his way.
Now, though, the burning heat of day,   4572
his heavy armor, did their worst,
so that his wounds now split and burst.
The bandages split, too, came loose.
Blood from his wounds was now profuse,   4576
and did not stop. He rode with speed,
back to where he had left Enide.
    She saw him, and her joy was great.
She did not see his wretched state,   4580
the pain he bore as best he could.
His body was all bathed in blood,
his heart, so weakened, seemed to fail.
Down a small hill and down a dale   4584
he rode; pitched forward on his horse;

falling upon its neck, perforce,
and struggling to regain his seat.
And now his stirrups left his feet,   4588
he fell, unconscious, as if dead.
What anguish started up, what dread,
in poor Enide, who saw him fall,
in pain and terror saw it all!   4592
She runs like those who can't conceal,
and won't, the wretchedness they feel,
and wrings her hands and shrieks aloud.
Not modest now, or poised, or proud,   4596
she tears her garments at the breast;
she tears her hair like one obsessed,
scratching her tender face and brow.
"Ah, God," she says, "fair, sweet sire, now   4600
why let me live? Why nourish me?
Take me, sweet Death; I yield to thee."
She falls upon the corpse and faints,
revives, with passionate complaints: 4604
"Alas!" she says, "poor wretch, Enide,
the killer of your husband! Deed
of madness, deed of idiocy!
He'd be alive if not for me,   4608
if not for the outrageous word
I, poor mad creature, told my lord.
Thus he is silenced now, cut down.
Judicious silence harms no man,   4612
while speech may harm him utterly.
This is the truth essayed by me,
oh, what a valiant proof is here!"
    Beside her lord and chevalier   4616
she sits, her head upon her knee,
and weeps in guilt and agony.
"*Haï!* Ill done, done wretchedly!

No man was equal, sire, to thee.   4620
Thou wert the form in Beauty's glass,
the proof, the form too, of Prowess,
had Wisdom's heart, and the fair crown
of noble Largess for thine own,   4624
without which one is of small price.
Poor judgment, and the ruinous vice
of pride caused me to speak, and led
my lord astray. Here he lies dead;   4628
venom my words, they poisoned him.
And I must answer now for them.
Oh, God! I recognize, I see
he would be living, but for me.   4632
I, I, must bear the blame alone!"
    Again she fell down in a swoon,
again awakened, tried to rise,
repeated, more and more, her cries.   4636
"Ah, God! Ah, why must I live on!
Death, dilatory, will not come,
but lingers, thwarts my respite. Why?
Death has great scorn for such as I;   4640
too proud, she will not condescend.
I must myself make my own end,
avenge my fault, champion the right.
And thus I die; I die in spite   4644
of Death, who would all help deny.
To call on Death is not to die;
complaints will bring Death's further scorn.
The sword which my seignior has worn   4648
will justly now avenge his death;
I will no longer waste my breath
on wishes, prayers, but keep my word."
    Now from its place she drew the sword,   4652
and she began to study it.

God slowed her movements just a bit,
He who is merciful and wise.
For while she made these dreadful cries,   4656
so full of pain and wretchedness,
now with much speed and much address
a count, with cavalry, appeared,
who, from a great way off, had heard   4660
her shrieks of anguish and regret.
This lady God did not forget;
she would have wreaked her own demise,
but the knights took her by surprise,   4664
seized the sword from her hands, and then
returned it to its place again.
And now dismounted, curious,
the count, who was solicitous   4668
to know: Who was the knight? Was she,
herself, his wife, or his *amie*?
"Both at once, simultaneously,
fair sire; but speech comes hard to me,   4672
it pains me that I am not dead."
    The count bade her be comforted.
"Lady," he said, "I beg, I pray,
have pity on yourself, I say!   4676
It's only right. Please, some relief;
nothing is gained by all this grief,
hysteria, and negligence.
Comfort yourself; it's common sense.   4680
Joy will be yours in time, and then
God give you happiness again.
Your beauty, splendid, rich, and great,
destines you for a better fate.   4684
I'll take you for my wife, and then
countess you'll be, and chatelaine.
Be comforted by such a word.

Now I shall have the corpse interred   4688
and with great honor laid in earth.
Leave off! Such grief's of little worth.
It's madness, how you carry on."
"Sire," she responded, "go! Begone!   4692
For God's sake, go, and let me be!
Nothing you do can influence me;
nothing you offer, speak or say
can give me joy in any way."   4696
   Now the count turned around and said:
"Make up a bier, men, for the dead;
we'll bear this corpse. And I will lead
the lady here. Come, we'll proceed   4700
straight to Limors, and expedite
the speedy burial of this knight.
Then I shall marry her at once,
regardless of her preference.   4704
Not in my life have I laid eyes
on so delectable a prize.
What joy to have discovered her!
Now, let us quickly make this bier,   4708
one that our horses can transport;
no slacking, men, of any sort."
At once they drew their swords, and laid
two cut logs parallel, and made   4712
of branches set across, a bed.
And now Erec—the honored dead—
between two horses was conveyed.
Near him Enide rode, sick, afraid,   4716
not ceasing from her grief at all.
Now she would faint, and now she'd fall,
and then the knights who led her came,
caught her up in their arms again,   4720
and held her up upon her horse.

They bore the body to Limors,
up to the palace of this count.

UP ON THE walls the people mount: 4724
knights, ladies, bourgeois, crowd the place.
In the main hall, upon a dais,
they lay the corpse with willing hands,
and next to it the shield and lance.   4728
The room is filled, great is the press;
they all ask questions, push and press.
What wonder here? What sad event?
    Meanwhile, in council now, the count   4732
speaks with his barons privily.
"Sires," he says, "now, immediately,
I wish this woman to receive.
My lords, you surely can perceive   4736
her beauty and her savoir faire,
her lineage, both fine and fair;
her looks and her nobility
are of such rank that easily   4740
in some great empire she'd be first.
With her I shall be none the worse;
indeed, my valor shall increase.
Fetch here my chaplain, if you please;   4744
you, bring the lady here at hand.
I mean to give her half my land
as dowry, if she'll do my will."
They bring the chaplain; they fulfill   4748
the count's commands, and bring him out.
And the poor lady, too, is brought;
they carry her along by force.
She struggles and protests, of course.   4752
He marries her without ado,

this count, just as he chooses to,
and makes his expeditious match.
The constables come, with dispatch;   4756
the tables, placed against the wall,
they set up in the palace hall,
quickly the evening meal prepare.
It's suppertime now, to be sure.   4760
    Vespers is over. Poor Enide,
on this May evening, is indeed
in great dismay and constant pain.
Now the count presses her again,   4764
often, with pleas and menaces.
Be at peace, love; rejoice, he says.
Upon a faldstool, or a throne,
she's placed; against her will it's done.   4768
Willing or not, she's seated there;
a table's placed in front of her.
The count is seated by her side;
his anger rises like a tide   4772
because he cannot comfort her.
"Lady," he says, "you must defer
and set aside all this distress.
Great pride and honor, happiness,   4776
you'll have in all my wealth, and me.
Surely, dear lady, you can see
grief will not make the dead return.
Such things are never seen nor done.   4780
Remember from what poverty
you've come, to wealth and property.
You were once poor; now you are rich.
Think of the gifts of Fortune which   4784
unstintingly are showered on you,
Countess! Wealth, dame, and title, too.

See here: your former lord lies dead.
If rage and grief surge in your head, 4788
think you I feel a great surprise?
Oh, not at all! But some advice
I'll give to you, the best I know:
now I have married you, and so, 4792
in your new husband now rejoice;
be ruled now by my wiser voice.
Eat: I invite, admonish you."
"Sire, that I have no heart to do. 4796
Sire, while I live and breathe and think,
I will not eat, I will not drink,
till I see rise, and take his place
my lord who lies upon that dais." 4800
    "Lady, that cannot be: and sick,
mad, senseless, a poor lunatic,
you will be judged, if you speak so.
Your just deserts, I'm warning you, 4804
you'll get, if I hear more today."
She did not have a word to say;
she thought his threats of small account.
He struck her on the face, this count, 4808
and she cried out. The barons, all,
disgusted, cried out in the hall.
"Leave off!" they cried out. "Sire, for shame!
You have disgraced your own good name. 4812
What, strike a woman? Slap and beat
this lady when she will not eat,
like some low swine, some oaf, some lout?
Poor wretched dame, she sees laid out 4816
in piteous death, her own seignior!
We say: what blame is there in her?"
"Silence, at once, all of you sirs!

The dame is mine, and I am hers.   4820
I'll do with her just as I will."
    At that Enide could not keep still:
she never would be his, she swore.
And he jumped up, and struck once more.   4824
At that she shouted out a dare.
"*Ahi!*" said she, "I do not care
what thing you say to me, or do.
I fear no threats or blows from you;   4828
strike me and beat me if you must.
Be fierce! Be brave! In my disgust
I'll do no more for you, or less,
even if you, in hardiness,   4832
tear out my eyes with your own hands
and cut me into strips and strands."
    This loud dispute and fierce complaint
now stirred Sir Erec from his faint,   4836
as if from sleep. He woke up, dazed;
small wonder, he was much amazed
to see these people all around.
Much pain and anguish now he found,   4840
hearing his wife's voice raised in fear.
To the ground leaps our chevalier,
taking his sword up instantly.
Rage gives him courage; he can see   4844
at once, her true, beleaguered love.
Seeing her, fast as he can move
he runs, he strikes the heedless count,
brains him, and breaks his skull and front—   4848
no *défi*, no discussion here!
The blood and brains fly through the air.
    Over the tables, at this revel,
leap the men, sure that he's the devil   4852

got in among them. Not one knight
remains; the youths, the old and white,
run in their terror and dismay
as fast as they can get away,   4856
one after other, in their rout,
and the whole palace empties out.
Feeble and fierce, they cry, this host,
"Flee, flee, the dead man! Flee the ghost!"   4860
Great is the crowd, and great the press;
they push and shove, in eagerness
to flee, they jostle, hustle, squeeze.
Those in the rear will have no ease   4864
until they've thrust themselves in front.
All of them flee; they do not want
or dare to linger, or to yield
Erec now runs to take his shield,   4868
winds the strap round his neck at once;
and Enide runs and takes his lance.
Into the courtyard now they run;
no one is bold enough, not one,   4872
to challenge them. The folk believe
no knight is this, no man alive,
but devil, vicious demon, who
inside the corpse, makes it pursue.   4876
They flee; they run; Erec gives chase.
One person still is in the place,
a boy who at this time can think
to lead his horse and have it drink,   4880
a saddled, bridled animal.
Thus does a piece of luck befall.
Erec now makes a rapid course,
and the poor boy lets slip the horse;   4884
he's terrified out of his wits.

Now in the saddle Erec sits,
helps Enide to the stirrup, where
she can leap on the destrier,   4888
seating herself near to its neck
as she's commanded by Erec.
The destrier supports the two:
they find the portal, canter through,   4892
no man arrests them at this gate.
The castle is all desolate;
all mourn the count who has been killed.
No brave soul, lingering, is filled   4896
with valor or with vengeful mood.
The count's been murdered at his food,
and Erec bears his wife away,
embracing her assiduously.   4900
Against his heart he presses her,
and says: "Sweet sister, to be sure,
well you have proved your love for me.
Henceforth have no anxiety: 4904
I love you as I never have,
and I am sure now that your love
is perfect, all I might require.
Henceforth it will be my desire   4908
to live as we lived formerly—
at your commandment I will be.
If you have spoken ill to me,
I pardon it entirely,   4912
forgive it all, with all good grace."
Now one more kiss, one more embrace.
    Enide feels no malaise at this;
she does not mind his gentle kiss,   4916
her lord's assurances of love.
Swiftly now through the night they move,

they ride, as in a magic light;
the moon is shimmering and bright.   4920

℮𝔅𝔵

MEANWHILE, THE TALE has quickly spread.
What speedier, more like to spread
than rumors, or more quick with cues?
Now King Guivret has heard their news: 4924
a wounded chevalier, it's said,
was lying in the forest, dead,
with him a girl, a lovely wight,
who shimmered like a star with light,   4928
and shrieked and made a dreadful moan.
Both have been taken, both have gone,
carried off by the count Limors,
who had his men bear off the corpse,   4932
and planned to wed the dame by force.
She has resisted this foul course.
When Guivret hears that they've been seized,
to say the least, he is not pleased;   4936
he thinks of Erec instantly.
And he resolves to go and see
whether the lady can be found
and the corpse put into the ground   4940
if it's Erec, and honor done.
Now he calls out a thousand men—
knights, sergeants; he will have them take
the castle, he will have them make   4944
the count give up the corpse and dame,
or visit on him fire and flame.
    The moon is shimmering and bright;
his people, hurrying in its light,   4948

have helmets laced, and hauberks on;
the shields around their necks are slung.
Armed to the teeth they go, they ride.
Near midnight, Erec has espied   4952
this band. He'll be entrapped or killed,
or, in some dungeon, surely stilled,
he thinks. Then, quickly, by a hedge,
in the dark shadow of its edge,   4956
he has Enide slip off his horse.
Small wonder he's dismayed, of course.
"Lady," he says, "stay here. Lie low,
here, where your movements cannot show;   4960
wait till these people pass and go.
They must not see you. Who's to know
what they are after, what they are.
Let's hope they do not see us here;   4964
I do not see one place to hide
should they observe us, and decide
to injure us. I can't foresee
what harm they might intend for me.   4968
Surely, whatever their intent,
nothing will stop me or prevent,
whatever challenger appears,
my jousting without any fears.   4972
But I am weak and sore. God knows,
for all this pain I have good cause.
Now I will ride to meet this lot.
You stay well hidden in this spot.   4976
Make sure you are not seen, until
They've left you far behind. Stay still."
     Thus his directions and his plans.
But now rode up, with lowered lance,   4980
Guivret, who'd seen them from afar

but did not realize who they were;
a black cloud hid the moon and made
all dark beneath its heavy shade. 4984
Battered and weak, now, Erec was;
Guivret, recovered from the blows
Erec had dealt him with such force.
Now Erec will be mad, or worse, 4988
not to show his identity.
Up from the hedge he gets, to see
Guivret come spurring, in fast fashion,
to meet Erec, without discussion, 4992
nor does Erec express his mood.
He thought to do more than he could.
When strength's unequal to ambition,
one must rethink, then, one's position, 4996
or perhaps let the matter rest.
Now each man rides; they fight; they joust;
but most unequal fight they seek:
one man is strong, the other weak. 5000
Guivret delivers with such force
that Erec tumbles from his horse,
over its rump. Enide, on foot,
sees her lord fall; he lies, stretched out, 5004
dead! They'll abuse his corpse! She flies
out from the hedge, throws off disguise,
runs to assist her dead seignior.
Her pain was great; now, how much more! 5008
She runs to Guivret, grabs his rein,
calling out to him in her pain:
"Evil knight, and despicable!
This is a weakened man, and sole, 5012
suffering, wounded mortally,
whom you attack. Such bravery!

This speaks of valor, what you've done?
If, without comrades, all alone,   5016
you had assailed him, you accursed,
you'd know how he could do his worst!
Oh, that he had his health again!
Sire, if you are a courteous man,   5020
be noble and be fair. Let drop
this battle that you've taken up.
What does your reputation gain
if you have overcome, or slain,   5024
a knight so weak he cannot rise?
Such is he; do but use your eyes.
See how the wounds he's suffered cover
body and limbs; blows, wounds, all over."   5028
    "Oh, lady, have no fright," said he.
"I see how well, how loyally
you love your seignior; I commend
your faith. Oh, fear me not, sweet friend,   5032
me, or my company of men,
in large things or in small. Now, then,
who is your lord? What is his name?
It's for his profit, my dear dame;   5036
whatever his identity,
do speak; trust me; say then to me,
who the man is. Quit, then, and free,
you'll both be, of anxiety."   5040
He spoke thus: and Enide, assured,
briefly responded with this word:
"His name is Erec. I can't lie,
hearing you speak so courteously."   5044
    Joyfully now descends Guivret,
and throws himself at Erec's feet,
where, on the ground, the man lies prone.

"Sire, just to seek you, I have come;   5048
I have been riding toward Limors.
I thought you dead. I'd heard, the corpse
all armored, of a chevalier,
was taken up and carried there.   5052
Please realize, I received such word.
The count Oringle, so I heard,
did this: took up the knight, then tried,
disgracefully, to make his bride   5056
a woman found there with the body.
She scorned the count, though, did this lady.
Then, friend, I felt great urgency
to find this dame and set her free.   5060
If he did not at once hand over
you, and the dame, without palaver,
I'd hold myself of little worth
if I'd left him a foot of earth!   5064
I would not undertake this move,
you know, sire, but for my deep love;
I am your friend Guivret. Take thought;
if I have injured you, you ought,   5068
since I did not know who you were,
to give me pardon, swift and sure."
Now, at this word, the other man
sits up—he moves as best he can—   5072
and says: "Guivret, dear friend, arise.
And since you did not recognize
your man, be pardoned and be quit."

        Up at once rises King Guivret.   5076
Now Erec tells him his account
of how it was he killed the count,
Oringle, where he sat at table,
and then, in fleeing to the stable,   5080

recovered his own destrier,
while sergeant and proud chevalier
fled, shrieking all around the place:
"Flee, flee! The corpse, the ghost, gives chase!"   5084
How he was almost snared, and then
escaped the count's ferocious men.
This tale told, Guivret made reply:
"Sire, I've a castle quite close by.   5088
It's in a lovely, healthy site.
There, for your ease and cure, sir knight,
tomorrow I would lead you. There
all of these wounds will have good care.   5092
I have two sisters of great spirit;
well they can treat a wound and cure it.
They're lovely girls; they'll do you good.
Now, for tonight, I think we should   5096
lodge in this field, with all my host,
till morning, for a bit of rest
I know will stand you in good stead.
Here, I advise, we'll make our bed."   5100
"I'm all accord, sire," Erec says.
      They settle there and take their ease.
They've no objections to the place,
but it is hard to find a space   5104
to lie; this gathering is not small.
Close by the hedges they sit, all.
Now the king Guivret's pavilion
is raised, and he has fuel brought on   5108
and fire made, to illuminate
the dark field. From the chests they take
the candles, and light up the tent.
Much less, now Enide's discontent;   5112
things have turned out much for the best.

Erec she's disarmed and undressed,
and she herself has washed his wounds,
dried them, and then replaced the bands;   5116
she will let no one else approach.
She knows Erec has no reproach;
he's put her to the test; she's passed;
he's sure of her great love at last.   5120
Guivret's great kindness, too, he knows.
Quilted cushions he's brought, pillows,
and made a bed both long and high,
with reeds and grass where one can lie.   5124
There, covered well, the knight can rest.
Now Guivret opens up a chest
and brings out from it three small pies.
    "Friend," he says, "have one. I advise   5128
a bit of this cold pie; a bit
of wine with water mixed with it.
Seven good barrels of wine I've got,
but pure wine's not for you; it's not   5132
healthy for such a wounded man.
My fair, sweet friend, now, if you can,
try; eat; for it will do you good.
Madame will also eat; she should,   5136
your wife, who for your sake today
has had such great anxiety.
You've come out well; you've cause to boast;
and you've escaped with nothing lost.   5140
Eat now, dear friends, and I will, too."
Beside him Erec sat, to do
just what was asked; thus he was eased.
And Enide sat; she was most pleased   5144
with all the efforts of Guivret.
Both of them urge the knight to eat

and drink the watered wine, which, pure,
would have been much too strong, that's sure.   5148
Erec ate like an invalid;
drank little; what he dared, he did.
He rested easily, and slept
near perfectly, all night; they kept   5152
noise down. They rose at break of day,
quick to take horse and ride their way.
Erec, who dearly prized his mount,
would hold no other of account.   5156
Enide was given a mule, for she
had lost her palfrey. One could see
no sign she minded what she got,
or that she had a worried thought.   5160
She had a handsome mule; its gait
was good; with ease it bore her weight.
She was much comforted to see
Erec had no anxiety,   5164
and seemed sure of recovery.

AT A STRONG castle, Pointurie
—indeed a healthy, lovely spot—
they came, at terce; found what they sought.   5168
There lived, with ease and with delight,
both Guivret's sisters, since this site
was so inviting and so fair.
Now, to a lovely chamber, where   5172
noise was far off, and where the air
was sweet and pure and healthful, there
Guivret led Erec. There the two
nurses began what well they knew.   5176
Painstakingly, they did their best,
following King Guivret's behest.

Erec had every confidence
in all their skill and competence.   5180
First, the dead flesh these two remove,
put on fresh bandages and salve;
with all their skill and all their care,
these two employed their savoir faire.   5184
Often they washed and cleaned the wounds,
wrapped them in ointment and fresh bands.
Each day, four times or more, they got
the knight to eat and drink a bit.   5188
No garlic would they let him eat,
or pepper. But of those who met
and left, passed in and out that way,
it was Enide who, every day,   5192
was with him, she who cared the most.
Guivret came often; gracious host,
asking about his wounded guest,
wanting to know his least request.   5196
He was well cared for and well served;
had he a wish, it was observed.
Had he a need, it surely was
met with a cheer most courteous.   5200
So conscientious in their ways,
his nurses, after fifteen days
he felt no illness and no pain.
To get his color back again   5204
they began bathing him. No leech
need lecture these two maids, or teach
their job to them, so great their skill.
    When he could come and go at will,   5208
Guivret had loose robes made, a pair
—one trimmed with ermine, one with vair—
of different silks. One, violet blue,
of *osterin;* and one, *bofu,*   5212

and striped; that one was a bequest,
his cousin's, up in the northwest
of Scotland. Enide had the gown
of ermine and of *osterin*.   5216
It was a garment rich and rare.
Erec wore the *bofu* with vair,
no less a thing of worth and wealth.
Now Erec has full strength and health;   5220
now he has manly force again.
And now his wife cannot complain;
she has her joy and her delight.
Now in their bed they play at night,   5224
wrapped in each other's arms, they kiss;
nothing can please them quite like this.
Evil and grief they've suffered; he
for her sake, and most certainly   5228
she for his. Now there's recompense.
Each with the other makes attempts
most valiantly, and vies to please —
Enough. My talk of this must cease.   5232
Now is their former pain forgotten,
and a new, greater, love begotten;
old pain sunk in oblivion.
    Now they must up and ride; move on.   5236
Thus they took leave of King Guivret,
who'd done so much, who'd been so great
a friend, performed all that he could
of honor, service, all that's good.   5240
And so Erec made his request:
"Sire, I must no more be your guest,
and tarry here, but seek my land.
Have prepared, then, and brought to hand   5244
all that is needed, all supplies.

I wish, at morning, at sunrise,
to be well started on my way.
So long, my friend, has been my stay   5248
that I feel hale again, and strong.
God willing, let me live so long
that we two, at some future hour
meet, and God grant I have the power   5252
to honor you, and to repay
your service. I'll have no delay,
I think, unless some enemy
sets upon me and captures me,   5256
before I come to Arthur's court.
There, I hope, if I've true report,
to find all gathered at Quarrois
or Caraduel, if that's the place."   5260
    Guivret has thoughts, though, of his own.
"Sir knight, you shall not go alone.
I shall go with you, and with me,
lead an assembled company   5264
—good men—if that's your will, fair sire."
With this advice and this desire
Erec is in accord; but wants
to see the plans he's made advance.   5268
That night they make all ready, for
he does not want to tarry more;
all is equipped, made fit and tight.
Early they rise, to expedite   5272
their plans; they saddle up the mounts.
Before they go, though, Erec wants
to seek the sisters in their room
and say farewell. And after him   5276
Enide comes running, merry-hearted
that they're now ready to get started.

They tell the sisters their goodbyes;
Erec, well-bred and civilized,   5280
tells of his gratitude at length,
for these two gave him life and strength.
He vows them service, like a knight,
and takes one by the hand, to plight   5284
this vow, the girl that nearest stands,
and Enide takes the other's hand.
They walk out of the room again,
all hand in hand, a festive chain.   5288
Up to the palace hall they stride.
   Guivret would have them mount and ride
with no more fuss, immediately.
And Enide wonders if she'll see,   5292
ever, this party rise and mount.
A palfrey's brought her, excellent,
soft-gaited, well made, finely bred.
Up to the mounting block it's led.   5296
Sound was this horse, and beautiful;
no less a worthy animal
than that abandoned at Limors.
This one was black; the other horse   5300
was sorrel. Its distinctive face
was strangely marked, by Nature's grace.
One cheek was white, like fresh, clean snow;
the other black as any crow;   5304
down the nose lay a lovely line
more green than leaves upon the vine,
a stripe dividing white from black.
One other truth you must not lack: 5308
saddle, breast piece, and harness, all
were fine work, artful, beautiful.
Breast straps and harness straps all held

bright heavy rows of emerald;   5312
the saddle, most original,
a purple, rare material;
the saddlebows of ivory,
on which was carved the history   5316
of how Aeneas fled from Troy,
and how, at Carthage, with great joy,
Dido received him in her bed;
how he deceived her, then, and fled,   5320
and how, for him, she took her life.
How he then conquered, with such strife,
Laurentum and all Lombardy;
all his life he held sovereignty.   5324
Finely carved, skillful work, it told
its tale in lineaments of gold.
A Breton artist sculpted it.
For seven years he put his wit   5328
to this task only, nothing else.
Whether he sold it no one tells;
dazzling would be its worth and cost.
Thus, for the palfrey that she lost,   5332
Enide had compensation sure,
when with this mount they honored her.
It was a present rich and rare,
with all its splendid, shining gear;   5336
she mounted, joying in her gift.
Now, too, there mounted, no less swift,
each good squire and each great seignior.
Tiercels and sparrow hawks they bore;   5340
many had goshawks, not yet mewed,
or *gruiers,* that hunt cranes for food.
And many hunting dogs they brought,
greyhounds and *brachets.* King Guivret   5344

in courtly knowledge not so short,
ordered them brought, for joy and sport.

e₿⚡

MORNING TILL VESPERS, thus they rode,
taking the fastest, straightest road,   5348
thirty Welsh leagues they went, and more,
until they found themselves before
a castle. Strong and beautiful,
it was girt round by a new wall,   5352
and also round this splendid keep
there ran a river, swift and deep,
and, stormlike, roaring on its course.
Seeing it, Erec stopped his horse,   5356
to look about and to inquire
who might be chatelain and sire
here, or what knowledge he could get.
"Friend," he said to the good Guivret,   5360
"this lovely castle that we see;
do you know, can you say to me,
what is its name? Have you such word?
Whose is it? Tell me, is its lord   5364
some count, or is the man a king?
Since you have brought me here, now bring
some knowledge to me. Speak, and tell."
"Sire," said Guivret, "I know it well.   5368
Truth you shall have, the full extent:
This castle is called Brandigant.
Lonely it is, and so secure
it fears not king nor emperor.   5372
If all the kingdoms round, if France
were to attack it, not a chance

they'd have; if all the realms from Liege
to here, surrounded it in siege,   5376
not in their lives they'd violate
so rich a realm, so strong and great.
Far more than fifteen miles extends
the isle on which this castle stands;   5380
and in its fields there grow and breed
all that a rich estate might need —
fruits, grains, fine wines, all earthly goods.
Nor do they lack fair streams and woods.   5384
In no part do they fear assault;
no enemy would starve them out.
King Evrain had it fortified;
he it is holds these lands so wide.   5388
Hold them he will, for all his days,
while in him life and breath have place.
He did not fortify for fear
of any foe that might appear;   5392
it makes the castle elegant.
Walls and towers, in any event,
make not a bit of difference,
but this great river's the defense,   5396
circling the island. Strong and sure,
they fear no man, but stand secure."
    "God!" said Erec, "what loveliness,
what might! We must see this fair fortress,   5400
and take our hostel here this night.
Here I intend, sire, to alight."
"Sire!" said Guivret, in pain. "Don't fault
me, friend, or think me difficult.   5404
Here, sire, we do not dare alight!
Here is a dreadful, evil rite!"
"Evil!" Erec replies. "How so?

Tell me about it, if you know,   5408
for all you know I wish to share."
"Sire," said Guivret, "I would have fear
that some great harm would come to you.
I know your courage!—boldness, too,   5412
and excellence. If now I were
to tell you of this *avanture,*
hardship and danger, every bit,
I have no doubt you'd follow it.   5416
Often I've heard this bit of lore:
that for full seven years or more,
of all who've followed this concern
not one has been known to return.   5420
From many lands, these chevaliers;
they are brave men, and proud and fierce.
Sire, do not take this as a jest!
More I'll not say, until I've pressed   5424
a vow on you, for dear love's sake
—such is my fear—that you'll not take
this road. No one escapes, no man.
Shame and death—only those are won."   5428
    Erec, who hears this with great cheer,
begs his friend leave off grief and fear,
and says: "My fair, sweet friend, *haï!*
Let us take hostel here, and see   5432
this castle, if you do not mind.
High time it is, sire, that we find
our lodging. If you'll not be pained,
possibly honor will be gained   5436
by both of us, and help our fame.
Of this *avanture,* tell the name—
just that, fair friend; no more of it.

And of the rest I'll hold you quit."   5440
"I'll do your pleasure," said Guivret.
"I'll not keep silence over that.
It is a lovely name to name;
it is the act gives grief and shame,   5444
for none escapes this *avanture*
alive and whole. Friend, I abjure:
'Joy of the Court' is the name they give."
"God! What, save good, can joy achieve?"   5448
says Erec. "Here's a route I'll take!
Now, do not go and, for my sake,
discourage me in this affair;
this one or any other, fair   5452
friend; we shall take hostel here.
Great good can come of it, that's sure.
Nothing can possibly detain me;
I'll seek this Joy You can't restrain me!"   5456
"Sire," says Guivret, "grant that God hears!
Grant that this Joy you do make yours,
returning without injury.
We must go in; this much I see.   5460
Since otherwise it may not be,
let us go, for our hostelry
is promised. There's no chevalier,
noble and great, or so I hear,   5464
wishing to enter through these walls
and ask for lodging in these halls
whom King Evrain does not receive.
So noble, he's been known to give   5468
this briefing to his townsfolk: none
should be a host to noble men.
Then he has opportunity,

himself, to honor royally   5472
all those good knights and noble hearts
who wish to come from foreign parts."
    Thus they come to this fair town's edge.
They pass the *lices* and the bridge;   5476
no sooner are the *lices* passed,
than all the townsfolk, who've amassed
there in the street, who crowd and mill,
see Erec, who's so beautiful,   5480
they seem to think, so much impressed,
this is the man who leads the rest.
All marveling, they stand and stare;
a tremor stirs the town. They share   5484
noisily, speech and conference.
Even the girls who sing and dance
leave off their carol and are still,
and, all together, look their fill,   5488
crossing themselves as they catch sight
of the great beauty of the knight.
Wondrous, the pity of each lass:
"God!" they say, each to each. "Alas!   5492
This chevalier whom we see pass
seeks the Joy of the Court, no less!
He will have sorrow all too soon.
No one from foreign countries, none,   5496
who comes to seek the dreadful Joy
but finds a shame that must destroy
honor and life. He'll end up dead;
forfeit, like all the rest, his head."   5500
Then they cry out, so he can hear,
raising their voices. "Chevalier,
ah, God defend you! Keep from all
horrors, a knight so beautiful!   5504

Beauty that is so pitiful!
Tomorrow it will all be null;
tomorrow, Death will blot you out,
oh, die you will, without a doubt,   5508
if God does not watch over you."
Erec heard all, and thus he knew
what they all said, throughout the town,
and seven thousand, up and down,   5512
mourned him; but none caused him dismay.
He rode straight on, without delay,
making salute most debonair
to men and women standing there;   5516
the men and women both he greets.
Most stand in anguish and in sweats;
no doubt they have in their surmise
that death or shame will be his prize.   5520
They've but to see his countenance,
appearance, beauty, noble stance,
and all their hearts reach out to him,
fearing his ruin, his chagrin;   5524
knights, ladies, maids: they dread his pain.
    The news had come to King Evrain
that to his court a personage
was come, with a great entourage.   5528
His harness and accoutrement
made him appear a king or count.
Into the middle of the street
rode King Evrain; he came to greet   5532
his visitors. "Be welcome, all
lords, and good people, to this hall;
be welcome, do. Dismount and stay."
Dismount they did; immediately   5536
plenty of hands received each horse.

The king was not remiss, of course,
when he observed Enide ride near.
Now he salutes her with good cheer,   5540
and runs to help the dame descend;
taking her fair and tender hand
he leads her to the palace thus,
as courtesy decrees he must,   5544
in every way he honors her,
for well he can such gifts confer.
Folly or malice has no part.
He has prepared a room apart   5548
with incense, aloes, and with myrrh;
great praise they gave, each traveler,
at what a lovely room they found.
And so they enter, hand in hand;   5552
the good king guides them, and displays
great joy in showing them this place.
Why dwell on details of the case? —
the silken hangings' gleaming grace,   5556
the exquisite embroidery —
that would be squandering foolishly
the time I do not wish to waste.
Indeed, I wish to make some haste,   5560
for he who keeps the road that's straight
soon passes those who deviate,
and thus I will not linger here.
King Evrain has his folk prepare   5564
the supper, for the hour has come.
That subject I'll not loiter on,
but keep the straight road, as I wish.
That night they served up every dish   5568
that heart could want or palate crave;
venison, fowl, and fruit they have,

and wine of many kinds is here;
but above all there is good cheer.　　　　5572
Always this is the sweetest fare;
good cheer and faces gay and fair.
　　Much were they served, and joyously.
Then Erec left off, suddenly,　　　　5576
putting aside his food and drink.
Now it was he began to think
of what his heart was set upon;
the Joy, which must be seized and won.　　　　5580
Hear now his speech, an urgent one,
what, with Evrain, was said and done.
"Sire," he began, "high time it is
that I declare to you the cause　　　　5584
that brought me here, on which I'm bent.
Too long I have been reticent;
now let my speech be quick and short.
I seek the Joy, sire, of the Court;　　　　5588
nothing else means so much to me!
Grant it, whatever it may be,
if you have power to do this thing."
"Surely, fair friend," replied the king,　　　　5592
"you speak great foolishness to me.
This task is one of agony
that has racked many worthy men.
You yourself will be, in the end,　　　　5596
destroyed; shamed, ruined, you will die,
if my good counsel you deny.
If you would place your confidence
in my advice, sire, you'd renounce　　　　5600
this ghastly favor that you ask.
You will not win out in this task.
Oh, speak of it no more! Be still!

You'll show no wisdom if you will   5604
refuse the counsel which I speak.
I do not wonder that you seek
honor and fame. But if I see
you seized and injured bodily,   5608
fair sire, it will torment my heart.
Believe me, I have seen depart
from here, fine men—each man my guest—
who make the Joy their urgent quest,   5612
all ruined. None of them profited:
all of them perished; all were dead.
By nightfall, by tomorrow's date,
you may expect just such a fate,   5616
if, as you wish, you seek this Joy;
have it you shall, but horribly!
It is a thing that, should you please,
you can withdraw from now with ease,   5620
if you would serve your interests well.
I say this to you; not to tell
the truth in its entirety
would be betrayal. It would be   5624
evil, fair friend, and false indeed."
  Erec, who listens, can concede
there's reason in the king's advice.
The wonder, though, he feels increase,   5628
the grave risk of this *avanture,*
and more and more he feels its lure.
He says: "Sire, I must say to you,
I find you loyal, wise, and true.   5632
I do not blame you, or accuse
you, in this course I wish to choose,
whether I win the day or lose.
But I'm resolved. Do not refuse!   5636

When on a plan my mind is set,
I do not shrink, a recreant,
but summon all my strength, and yield
only when I must flee the field."   5640
"I know that," said the king, "but still,
I grant this boon against my will.
The Joy that you require of me
I grant, with much anxiety   5644
and much despair; I sense mischance.
In this, at least, have confidence:
I shall bestow what you desire.
If you have Joy of it, fair sire,   5648
you shall have won great honor, more
than any man's won heretofore.
And may God, as I wish, bestow,
a joyous victory on you."   5652
    Late into evening, they talk
of Erec's quest, until the folk
go to the beds prepared for them.
Next morning, soon as day has come,   5656
Erec, the ever-watchful one,
sees the clear dawn, he sees the sun,
and rises from his bed to dress.
Enide lies there in great distress;   5660
her sorrow and anxiety
all night have gripped her cruelly,
in apprehension and in fear.
The lord she loves and holds so dear   5664
seeks out a fate so perilous.
He stands there, all preparedness;
no one can stop him. Now the king,
to fit out Erec, has men bring   5668
arms which Erec puts to good use.

They are no gift he will refuse,
for his own arms are too much worn,
battered and damaged, bent and torn;   5672
willingly now he takes these all,
and he is armed there in the hall.
    Armed, he descends the steps; and there,
saddled, he finds his destrier,   5676
and the king mounted on his steed.
Others mount up now, with due speed.
They come from court, they come from inn;
throughout the town, there's none within,   5680
able to go, who does not stir.
Now, at the start, there is uproar,
shouting in all the streets, and noise:
nobles and menials, with one voice   5684
all crying out, "*Haï! Haï!*
Oh, chevalier, lured wretchedly
by Joy—and, you think, Victory—
Death you win; death, in agony."   5688
Not a soul stood there, or drew breath,
but cried, "God curse you, Joy! This death
you've given knights so excellent!
Today, this day, brings an event   5692
worse, worse than all, without a doubt."
Now Erec hears them, and takes note
how they all talk, and mourn, each one.
"Friend," they say, "how wretchedly done,   5696
this act of yours; oh, handsome knight,
so noble, skillful, and adroit!
It seems to us against all right
your life should be so soon forfeit,   5700
that mortal suffering so great,
and mortal hurt, should be your fate."

He hears these words, and what they've said:
never does he incline his head,   5704
but passes on his outward way.
Nothing in him seems cowardly.
Eager he seems, to sense, to see
what is their great anxiety,   5708
their terror and their suffering.
   Out from the castle now the king
leads him. There is an orchard near.
They follow, all, the chevalier,   5712
praying that God will give them heed,
and bestow Joy upon their need.
But I must not continue on,
weary and feeble in my tongue,   5716
but give this orchard's history
in all its grim veracity.
No stake, or pale, or wall was there;
the only boundary seemed the air.   5720
But this same air was, by some trick
of necromancy, dense and thick.
Nothing could come into this place
unless it sought out one sole space;   5724
iron walls might have circled it.
In winter's cold and summer's heat
fruit and blooms grew continually.
This fruit had a strange property: 5728
There, one could eat it; if one tried
to carry any fruit outside,
he would be thwarted; he would learn
he was not able to return—   5732
escape was gone, his former route
cut off—till he replaced the fruit.
No bird that flies beneath the sky,

singing, delighting with its cry   5736
all humans, making them rejoice,
was absent; one could hear each voice,
exultant, individual.
This earth, while it exists at all,   5740
does not support one herb or spice
or thing that man has made suffice
for cordial, remedy, or cure
that did not bloom and flourish there.   5744
    Now singly, through the aperture,
so narrow, came each follower—
the king first, then his countrymen.
Erec now placed himself, and then   5748
held his lance in its sock, at rest,
heard the birds shout, from twig and nest:
The Joy! The Joy! Songs, noisy wings,
harbingers and foreshadowings   5752
of what he longed for most of all.
But what a horror, past that wall!
Surely it would have terrified
anyone venturing inside,   5756
brilliant Thibaut li Esclavons
or all whose reputations
we know—Opiniax; Fernaguz—
for there stood stakes with fearsome views: 5760
a glittering helmet on each top,
under each helmet ring, a crop
of ghastly fruit—a dead man's head.
Except for one stake; there, instead,   5764
no grisly flower or fruit stood yet,
but a horn, only, had been set.
    Erec observes, but has no sense
of this strange scene's significance;   5768

no fear. Evrain rides at his right;
and Erec asks, "What means this sight?"
And the king listens, and replies:
"Fair friend, do you not realize   5772
what it is stands here, what you see?
Oh, you will feel anxiety,
cold, gripping fear! Does your body
mean nothing to you? Now, hear me: 5776
Look at that horn there, on that stake.
Long it has hung there, for the sake
of some brave knight, we know not who,
some other chevalier, or you.   5780
Take care that your head is not lost,
and thrust upon that waiting post,
designed for it! You've been warned well,
before you came! Oh, I can tell   5784
you will not leave this horrid court;
you will be killed and cut apart.
Well, now you know the chance you take:
your head will sit there on that stake.   5788
And if this happens, as it must
—for that's the bargain—you have lost
your life for nothing. This thing done,
another stake will be put in,   5792
in place of yours, and it will wait
for some unknown to find his fate.
I will say nothing of the horn,
for none of us has heard it blown;   5796
we cannot do it. He who can,
we will prize over any man
in our estate; and all who live
will think his worth superlative,   5800
honor him as the best of us,

most brave, and most illustrious —
ah, well, there's nothing more to say.
Bid all your people go away.   5804
The Joy awaits this rendezvous,
and will, I think, bring pain to you."
    King Evrain turned and left at this.
Now Erec gave Enide a kiss.   5808
Beside him, with heart fit to break,
she stood; of pain she would not speak,
for grief that face and voice impart
means nothing; true grief's from the heart.   5812
Erec, who knew so well her thought,
now said: "Sweet sister, why such doubt?
My gentle, loyal lady, she
whom I prize for sagacity!   5816
Your fear is great, I can see that.
My love, I do not know for what.
For nothing, this anxiety,
until, my dearest one, you see   5820
my shield all broken, every bit,
me lying wounded under it,
my hauberk stained, not white, but red,
the bright links covered with my blood,   5824
my helmet smashed and torn and rent,
and me defeated, fearful, spent,
all my defenses smashed, lost, gone,
praying for mercy, all undone,   5828
against my will a suppliant —
then you may well make this lament.
But you begin too soon, lady!
Sweet love, you don't know what's to be;   5832
nor yet do I, and all this care
means nothing; nothing, all this fear.

You know; you know so certainly,
if there is hardiness in me,   5836
if there's such courage as your love
can stir, and make my spirit move,
I fear no fight, no man alive.
Joyously, hand to hand, I'll strive.   5840
This seems like foolish boasting. Dear,
I speak to overcome your fear,
not from false pride. Put dread away,
be comforted. I cannot stay.   5844
Alas, you may not come with me,
and now we must part company;
for this is King Evrain's decree."
He kissed her, and to God's mercy   5848
commended her. So, too, did she,
for him; still in anxiety,
because she could not ride and go,
follow, see for herself, and know   5852
this outcome, how he'd expedite
whatever task this was, or fight.
So she remained, to wait, to grieve,
since there was no alternative;   5856
sad, fearful of the aftermath.

EREC NOW RODE along a path,
companionless entirely.
A silver couch he soon could see,   5860
on which a gold-trimmed cloth was laid
under a sycamore's deep shade;
a *pucelle* sitting in that place
lovely of body and of face,   5864

all earthly beauties from her shone.
There sat this lady, quite alone.
I do not want to say much more,
but anyone observing her,   5868
her beauty, her attire, could say
that truthfully, in every way,
Lavinia of Laurentum,
gracious and fair, had not the sum   5872
—no, not a fourth—of her beauty.
Erec approached her side, to see
this beauty closely, study it;
at the girl's side prepared to sit.   5876
    But, watch! There comes a chevalier
straight through the orchard, riding near;
armed in vermilion arms, this knight,
huge, and a wondrous, monstrous sight.   5880
Aside from this enormity,
not under heaven could there be
a man so handsome. Now, this knight
was taller by a foot in height,   5884
so said all witnessing the scene,
than any other knight they'd seen.
He saw Erec; at once cried out,
"Vassal! Vassal! You witless lout!   5888
If I know much, you are a churl,
sidling and stalking up my girl!
You're not the man, sire, to my mind,
thus to approach; you're not the kind.   5892
By my head, you'll pay heavily,
and soon, for your stupidity.
Stand back!" He stopped, this chevalier,
and looked at Erec, who stood there,   5896
neither moved toward the other, till

Erec spoke up, and spoke his fill.
"Friend," he said, "in such arguments
folly is said as soon as sense.   5900
Menace and threaten all you please,
this man will stand here at his ease,
silent; in threats there's no good sense.
And why? The man whose arrogance   5904
has made him very sure he's won
can find he's lost, outclassed, outdone.
His threats then have a clownish grace.
Men often flee; as often chase.   5908
I'm not so fearful of your threat
that I'm about to flee just yet.
I'm ready now to match my might
with any man who'd seek a fight,   5912
and I'll pursue him with such force
he'll not escape by any course."
"No," said the other. "God me save!
Sire, be advised: this fight you'll have.   5916
I challenge you; I make *défi*."
    Listener, believe this fact of me:
neither held back his reins at all.
Nor were their lances light and small,   5920
but both were stout and thick and good,
rigid and strong, of well-cured wood.
Upon the shields, with all their strength,
they hurled their trenchant weapons' length,   5924
and as they rode, each chevalier
thrust a full fathom of his spear
through shields that flashed with brilliant light;
yet flesh was carved by neither knight,   5928
and neither rider broke his lance.
Each man, upon his earliest chance,

drew back his weapon, then once more
both rushed to the embrace of war, 5932
battling and jousting, knight with knight.
Fierce they are, wild, precise, adroit.
They ride, they strike; as they engage,
they break their lances in their rage, 5936
and under them their horses fall.
But they sustain no hurts at all,
those in the saddles; quick, they rise,
agile and brave and battle-wise. 5940
On foot, beneath the trees, these men
strike with their good steel swords from Vienne;
such powerful, hurtful blows each knight
struck on the flashing shields, the bright 5944
bucklers broke up and cracked in fours.
How their eyes shone! The warriors
now strove their best to wreak their worst,
to give most grief, and give it first, 5948
laboring in their battle thirst
and straining. Both, in wrath immersed,
thrust at each other and attacked.
Wildly they thrust and hewed and hacked, 5952
now with the flat part of the blade,
now with the cutting edges played.
They hammered at each other's teeth,
noses, and cheeks, and flesh beneath, 5956
at fists, and arms, and plenty more,
temples, napes, necks; their bones are sore.
Sore, wretched, tired, no recreants,
these two do not give up the dance, 5960
but fiercer, faster, each one tries.
Sweat drips, and irritates their eyes—
sweat and the drops of blood that fall,

so that they hardly see at all. 5964
Often their strokes now go astray,
so that they cannot see the play
of swords, direct it, cannot see
to give each other injury. 5968
Listeners, you must not doubt, however:
there was no slack in their endeavor;
they do not let their strength give way.
Blinded and stumbling in the fray, 5972
their eyesight now completely gone,
they drop their shields and still fight on,
still with great rage in their attack:
they drag each other forth and back, 5976
now on their knees they slash and beat.
　　Thus a long time these warriors meet,
until the hour of noon has passed.
Then the great chevalier, at last, 5980
is out of breath; he gasps and sighs.
At Erec's mercy now he lies;
Erec now drags and pulls the laces
of the knight's helm; they fall in pieces. 5984
Across Erec he falls, and lies
upon his chest; he cannot rise,
and face down in the earth, the man
now lies engulfed in his chagrin: 5988
sue he must, vanquished in this trial.
"Sire, you have conquered. No denial
is possible. Harsh, hateful chance!
However, speak; if now perchance 5992
your prowess and your name are great,
there will be honor in my fate.
Could I then beg of you, and pray
this favor, sire; is there no way 5996

that I might learn, at last, your name,
and have some comfort in my shame?
Since, despite all, you've conquered me,
I shall rejoice, I guarantee,   6000
if you're a man of great renown;
if a worse man has cut me down,
then I face grief, and harsh self-blame."
"My friend, you wish to know my name,"   6004
said Erec. "You shall know it soon;
before I go, I'll grant your boon.
On one condition: you agree
here, now, at once, to say to me   6008
why you are at this orchard here.
From start to end I want to hear
your every word. Your name; this Joy—
I long to hear its history."   6012
"You shall know all; the truth, entire.
Fearlessly I will speak, fair sire;
all that you wish to hear, I'll say."
    Erec, well pleased, did not delay: 6016
"You've never heard, from anyone,
of King Lac and Erec his son?"
"Indeed, fair sire; well, I can say.
At King Lac's court I chanced to stay   6020
for many days, while still a squire.
If Lac had had his true desire,
I'd not have left, for anything."
"You stayed at court with Lac, the king?   6024
He is my father. You knew me,
well, if you stayed there; it must be."
"Faith! What a happy chance I've found!
Now, hear me. Hear how I've been bound,   6028
held, in this orchard—oh, so long!

As for my story, sire, I long
to tell it. Any cost I'll bear.
   "That girl whom you see sitting there   6032
loved me from childhood; and I, too,
loved her. Our love increased, it grew,
and our delight was mutual.
She asked me—how these things befall!—   6036
a boon she would not name to me.
What man refuses his *amie*?
Oh, if he does, no lover he,
who does not, with alacrity   6040
do his love's will, seize any chance
with no faint doubts of negligence!
And so I promised, with all speed,
to do her will; when I'd agreed,   6044
still she would have me swear an oath.
More I'd have done, in very truth,
anything; but she took my vow.
I swore; to what, I did not know.   6048
At last, in time, I was dubbed knight;
Evrain, my uncle, in the sight
of many a brilliant chevalier
knighted me in this orchard here,   6052
near where we stand. My sweetheart, she
who sits there, now recalled to me
my promise and my sacred oath
I'd sworn to her. I'd made my troth   6056
never to leave this place, this site,
until there came to me a knight
who, in armed trial, would vanquish me.
Oh, right demanded I agree!   6060
Rather than fail here in this troth,
I should have never sworn my oath.

Now in this lady I held dear
I knew, I saw, the good; and cheer,					6064
seeming delight, I had to show,
not my displeasure or my woe.
For if she sensed these, chanced to see,
she would withdraw her heart from me;					6068
oh, not for any price at all
would I have such a thing befall!
And so she thought, my demoiselle,
that a long sojourn, a long spell,					6072
I'd have here; there would be no day
when some fine vassal came this way,
entered this orchard, thrust me out.
All the days of my life, she thought,					6076
I'd be at her disposal, caught,
held in the prison she had wrought.
Oh, wrong it would have been, and shame,
if, over all the knights who came,					6080
I'd been remiss in victory!
Cheap, foul, would be such liberty,
when power was mine, and mine the chance!
Disgusting, such deliverance.					6084
I say to you: I had no friend
so dear, that were we to contend
in arms, I would scant all my skill,
or fail to force him to my will.					6088
Oh, you have seen those helmets! Those
of men I conquered by my blows,
and killed. Their deaths come not on me.
Look at right, reason, and agree—					6092
for to give no defense, I must
be false in faith, betray my trust.

"The truth I've told you; told it all.
Honors you've won by no means small,   6096
as you well know, in conquering me.
Now much rejoicing there will be,
and in my uncle's court, great cheer,
since now I'm free to go from here.   6100
Since there'll be such festivity,
and joy in court and company,
Joy of the Court is what they'll call
this joy, this longed-for festival.   6104
Oh, long has been their longing, great
their hope for this first time, their wait
for you to come, victorious.
Now you checkmate, enchant me thus,   6108
bewitch my might and chivalry.
Fitting and fair it seems to me
    I wish it—that you know my name.
I am, sire, called Maboagrain.   6112
But by that name I am not known
save in this country, this alone.
But go to any other place
where I've been seen, folk know my face,   6116
since I was vassal; you will find
folk do not keep this name in mind.
Now you know all the truth, fair sire.
My tale is told, as you require.   6120
Yet there is more; I must tell on.
Sire, in this orchard is a horn:
one you have seen, I do believe.
Fair sire, this place I may not leave   6124
until that horn is blown; the sound
dissolves my prison. Free, unbound,

I'll be; the Joy will start; and he
who listens and who hears shall be   6128
held to no hindrance. He may go,
when he has heard that voice, that blow,
at once to court, without delay.
Oh, rise up, sire! Go, straightaway,   6132
take the horn quickly, blow the blast!
Since nothing hinders you at last,
do what you must. Oh, blow the horn!"
    And now Erec is up and gone,   6136
and up and gone with him, his guide;
Both go together, side by side.
And Erec takes the horn and blows;
all of his strength and force he shows,   6140
and the sound bounds, falls, far away.
And Enide hears it joyously;
joyous the king, the folk. Not one
but celebrates the deed, now done,   6144
feels a deep pleasure in this thing.
They do not cease or rest, but sing,
make merriment and festive play.
Erec can truly boast this day   6148
that such great joy has never been;
it can't be told by mouth of man,
recounted well and truly, but
I'll give you the sum of it,   6152
briefly; no excess mouthing here.
    Through all the country, far and near,
news flies; all hear the outcome now.
None hesitates, none holds back; how   6156
they rush, the people, to the court!
They hasten, folk of every sort.
By foot, by horse, they push and scurry;

they forget others in their hurry. 6160
Those in the orchard press in flight
toward Erec, to disarm the knight.
Rivals, they strive in joy to sing
a song of festive fashioning; 6164
the dames, in their festivity,
invent a song, the Lay of Joy —
but this song's lost, it's not well known.
And Erec's joy has swelled and grown, 6168
and all his wants have been well eased.
    One person here is not well pleased:
the lady on the silver couch.
This Joy, she sees, will not do much 6172
to bring her pleasure. Still, it's sure
that many people must endure
what weighs upon them heavily.
Enide, though, showed great courtesy. 6176
She saw this pensive girl, who sat
alone upon her couch; she thought
at once to go to her and speak,
ask now her situation, seek 6180
to know her state, who she might be,
and something of her history,
unless this was too harsh a task.
She thought to go alone and ask, 6184
and lead no others; but then came,
following her, *pucelle* and dame,
most noble folk, and beautiful.
These women made a party, all, 6188
and for companionship, for love,
they gathered round, they sought to give
comfort, assurance, happiness
to her the Joy caused such distress. 6192

To this sad girl it seemed that she
must now live less with her *ami,*
much less than was her will and wont,
since he must leave this orchard haunt.   6196
Her great displeasure went for naught,
she could not stop him; that was that—
the time had come, the hour was here.
And this was why now many a tear   6200
streamed from her eyes, her face. Distress,
rage, more than I can well express,
she felt. However, up she rose,
stood straight and proud. Not one of those   6204
wishing to help, who now drew near
could reach her; she'd no wish to hear.
    Enide, in graceful, cheerful style,
greeted the girl. She, for some while,   6208
could speak no word, made no replies,
strangled and stopped by sobs and sighs,
which, in their fierceness, strength, and size,
shook her whole form in gasps and cries.   6212
Then, a long moment after that,
she returned Enide's greeting, but
regarded her with special care,
for a long moment studied her.   6216
This lady seemed familiar;
she'd known her, seen her face before,
she thought, not sure; when could that be?
Quickly, now, she made inquiry.   6220
Where was she from? What country? Where
was her lord born? She asked, who were
they, both? and urged Enide to say.
And Enide answered straightaway,   6224
recounted all, revealed the truth.

"That count," she said, "who holds Laluth
as his domain, he is the brother,
full-blood relation, to my mother.   6228
Born I was, nurtured in my youth,
niece to the count who rules Laluth."
    The other laughs. She can't resist
the joy she feels at hearing this;   6232
pain gone, heart full of joy, she feels
a gaiety no one conceals,
a joyousness she cannot hide.
She rises now to kiss Enide,   6236
throws her arms round her, says to her:
"I am your cousin. This is sure,
it's the whole truth. It is my father
you are niece to; it is his brother   6240
who is your own sire. But I doubt
much that you've ever heard about
how I came to this country here.
The count, your uncle, was at war;   6244
from many countries, many men
served, as hired soldiers, under him.
And so it happened, it was thus,
that one such mercenary was   6248
a chevalier from Brandigan,
and nephew to its king. This man
lived with my sire a year or so.
That was, I think, twelve years ago.   6252
I was a child still, and this knight
was handsome, valorous, adroit—
and so we made, we two, a troth
that was most pleasing to us both.   6256
I had no wish but his, and he
began, at long last, to love me;

he swore to be my man forever,
always to be my loyal lover,   6260
and lead me here. And I and he
were pleased by this trust equally.
He was impatient to depart,
and I, too, longed, with all my heart,   6264
to go with him. We came here, thus,
and no one knew of it but us;
you and I were both young and small.
Now I have finished. Tell me all,   6268
yourself, as you have heard from me,
the true tale of your own *ami,*
by what adventure did he win
you and your love? Speak!" "Fair cousin,   6272
he married me, all openly.
My father knew it was to be,
for certain, and my mother had
great pleasure in it. All were glad,   6276
of all our folk, as they should be.
The count, too, blessed us joyfully.
He has no need to prove his worth,
his valor, or his gentle birth.   6280
None of his generation can
match, in nobility, this man.
His love for me is great; my love
for him is greater. What we have   6284
between us could not be increased.
Never once have I failed or ceased
to love him as I must; for he,
a king's son, he has chosen me,   6288
a poor girl, naked, as I was.
Through him I have great honor thus.
Never did Christian man so clothe

the poor in splendor and in love.   6292
Now, if it pleases you, I'll say
—I will not lie—what was the way
I reached such heights. I won't delay—
no idle tale, this." Straightaway   6296
she told, in all detail and truth,
how Erec rode into Laluth.
She had no wish to hide detail,
but word for word she told her tale,   6300
left nothing out. I won't regale
you with it; you would think it stale,
hearing it twice. Thus they conferred.
    One lady in the group, who'd heard,   6304
hurried to let the barons know.
Thus did the Joy increase and grow.
They knew the Joy, they knew the word,
rejoicing, all, in what they heard;   6308
Maboagrain, especially,
above all, heard it joyfully,
for now his love was comforted.
And she who hurried off and spread   6312
the news so expeditiously
brought quick and sudden gaiety
to all; the king himself was glad.
He had been happy; now he had   6316
much greater reason than before.
    Enide now went to her seignior,
leading her new-found cousin, she
who surpassed Helen in beauty,   6320
eclipsed her, too, in charm and grace.
Now all came hurrying to that place,
to meet them; Erec, Maboagrain,
and Guivret, and the king Evrain,   6324

and all the others in their train,
to honor them. Now met again,
no one kept still or stayed behind!
Maboagrain, with joyful mind   6328
greeted Enide; she greeted him;
Erec and Guivret, both of them,
greeted the lady joyously.
With such a joy now, they and she   6332
made cheer and comfort, with what zest
fell on each others' necks and kissed!
They must go back to town, they said;
they had been in this dreadful glade   6336
too long; all wanted now to leave.
And thus they go, and going, give
joy, each to each; with kisses meet.

    They were all in King Evrain's suite;   6340
but as they traveled toward the town,
barons from all the country round
joined them, all knowing of the Joy.
All came who could come, possibly.   6344
Great was the crowd, and great the press;
they jostled in their eagerness
to see Erec—high, low, rich, poor.
Each pushes for a place before   6348
the others. Now they bow in greeting,
all of them endlessly repeating:
"God save this man, most fortunate
of all God labors to create!"   6352
Thus they lead Erec to the court.
Now, shouting, how they all disport
themselves, what joy and glee abound!
Harps, viols, Breton zithers sound,   6356
the symphonias and psalteries,

the stringed and fretted *armonies* —
more instruments than one could list.
But such details I must resist,   6360
not fuss and linger overmuch.
The king gave Erec honor, such
as kingly honor can bestow;
no others grudged him, or were slow   6364
to serve; eager they were, each one.
    Three days, it was, the Joy went on,
before Erec could get away.
But, came the fourth, he would not stay;   6368
no urgings heard, of any sort.
With joy they made him an escort,
crowded around him, taking leave.
All the farewells that he could give   6372
to all, would take full half a day,
if to each one he said goodbye.
He greeted and embraced the lords;
and to the others spoke fair words,   6376
gave them adieu and fair salute.
Enide, too, was by no means mute,
but to the barons did the same,
said her farewells to each, by name.   6380
They spoke as one to her. At last,
tenderly, closely, she embraced
and kissed her new-found cousin. Then
the two took leave; the Joy was done.   6384

ॐ

THEY LEFT; THE others went their way.
Erec and Guivret would not stay
at Evrain's court, but now took horse

joyfully, and with swiftest course   6388
came to the castle where, they'd learned,
King Arthur and his court sojourned.
King Arthur had been bled that day;
there with him, in the privacy   6392
of his own chambers, one could see
five hundred lords of his meiny—
a small, depleted number. Never,
at any season, had he ever   6396
felt so alone. Distressed he was,
there with so few lords of his house.
But now there comes in, hurrying,
a messenger, to tell the king   6400
that Erec and Guivret draw near;
he has been sent as herald here.
Quickly this messenger appears,
locates the king and chevaliers,   6404
salutes them all sagaciously.
"Sire," he says, "Hear this word from me:
Erec and Guivret come to court.
They come to see you." This report   6408
he offered to King Arthur thus.
"Most welcome are they here with us,
as barons wise and valorous,"
the king responded. "Nowhere does   6412
a better knight than these two live.
With them our court will surely have
much honor." He called Guinevere,
and gave this latest news to her,   6416
and others saddled up their mounts,
to go and meet these two at once.
None of them troubled with their spurs,
such eagerness to ride was theirs.   6420

Briefly I'll tell the sum of all
who stood outside the castle wall:
the gathered crowd of commoners,
waiters and cooks and cupbearers,   6424
to tend the lodgings, stew and bake;
the main cortege was in their wake,
following speedily, and soon
they had arrived, and were in town,   6428
with Arthur's party face-to-face.
How they all kiss then, and embrace!
Now at the inns they take their rest,
and of their traveling clothes divest   6432
themselves, and in rich garments dressed,
come to King Arthur's court at last.
Arthur receives them. Guinevere,
wild with delight and frenzied cheer,   6436
longs to hang on each loved friend's neck;
her dear Enide, her loved Erec.
Exultant, like some falcon, she!
Her joy is plain for all to see.   6440
All strive to welcome and to please,
until King Arthur orders peace,
for he wants news from Erec; wants
tales of his ventures, full accounts.   6444
And so Erec begins the tale;
recounts it, to the last detail,
forgetting nothing. You suppose
I'll spell out what his motive was,   6448
explain it all, my audience?
Oh, no; you've heard all these events,
the truth of them, and others, too.
I won't recount them all for you,   6452
that would be prolix, dull, *de trop,*

I'd be aggrieved at that, I know.
It's no brief tale. He who'd begin
must place each word most deftly in,   6456
as he toils through each episode.
First, the three worthies of the road,
whom Erec beat in combat; then
the five who followed; and, again,   6460
Count Caloain and his foul plot;
and then the giants, after that—
each piece in order, bit by bit,
Erec recounted all of it.   6464
At length he gave a full account
of how Limors, the vicious count
had his head broken at his dinner,
and Erec, once again the winner,   6468
got back his war-horse in the end.
    "Erec," the king said, "fair, sweet friend,
stay in this country; live here. Stay,
part of our court, as was your way."   6472
"Sire, if you wish it, I'll remain,
most willingly, at court again,
I'll gladly stay two years or three.
But I beg, sire, that here with me   6476
Guivret may live; and this I pray."
King Arthur urged Guivret to stay;
Guivret accepted. Both remained.
And the king gladly entertained   6480
and honored both, and held them dear.

*e*B*X*

THERE, FOR LONG, lived our chevalier
—Erec, Enide, Guivret together—

until the death of Erec's father, 6484
at a great age, when full of years.
Now they send out the messengers:
those who go seek him are the great,
proudest of barons in the state. 6488
They ride, they search, they seek, until
at last they come to Tintagel,
eight days before the festival
of Noel. Here at last, they tell 6492
Erec the truth; his father's gone,
the good, old, hoary king's passed on.
This news weighed much on Erec, though
he did not let his grieving show 6496
before his people, since a king
must not give way to sorrowing.
And there at Tintagel, he had
vigils and masses sung and said; 6500
his royal vows he kept now, all,
for every church and hospital.
All that one should do, he did well:
chose from the poor and miserable 6504
more than a hundred sixty-nine
whom he re-dressed, in clothing fine.
To the poor clerks, each needy priest,
he gave, as fitting, a pelisse, 6508
warm underneath, and a black hood.
For the Lord's sake, he did great good,
giving to those whose coins were scarce
more than a barrel of deniers. 6512
    With his wealth given in this wise
Erec performed a deed most wise:
from Arthur he received his land.
He begged his liege that he be crowned 6516

at Arthur's court; such was his prayer,
and the king told him to prepare
quickly, for both his wife and he
at the feast of Nativity,   6520
so close at hand, were to be crowned.
And he made also this command:
"Go, then, to Nantes, in Brittany,
with the ensign of royalty—   6524
the crown of gold, the scepter, too.
This honor I bestow on you."
Erec gave thanks; he told his liege
this was a noble privilege.   6528
    Then came the Christmas festival.
Assembled were the barons, all;
by order of the king, they came,
by order, too, was every dame   6532
commanded; none remained at home.
Erec decreed that many come,
and many followed that decree;
so many came, in fact, that he   6536
could not believe the crowd so great
that came to honor his estate.
I cannot tell you all who came,
or list each one, and speak each name,   6540
who was at court and who was not.
Two guests, for certain, weren't forgot:
Lady Enide's fair sire and dame.
He was the first of all who came,   6544
commanded there; magnificent,
he came to court for this event,
like a great chatelain and lord.
He brought no silly, gaping crowd—   6548
no bunch of chaplains milling there,

or simpletons to stand and stare,
but chevaliers, the first, the best,
well fitted out and bravely dressed.   6552
Each day they traveled quite some way,
rode, knights together thus, each day;
joyous and proud and elegant,
on Christmas Eve they came to Nantes.   6556
They did not stop or rest at all
until they entered the great hall.
    Erec and Enide saw them come,
and, without pausing, went to them,   6560
fell on their necks in glad embrace,
spoke their dear names with tender grace
and glad rejoicing, as was right.
Then, welcome done, with such delight,   6564
they took each other's hands, all four,
and, thus rejoicing, came before
Arthur, and did their homage there,
and, too, saluted Guinevere,   6568
who sat beside him. By the hand
Erec now took his host and friend
and said, "Sire, mark us: here you see
my gracious host, most dear to me;   6572
no one could be more courteous.
He made me lord of his own house,
before he knew me; offered me
all of his goods and property,   6576
even his daughter for my own.
And without counsel all was done."
"And this fair lady, whom I see
standing beside him; who is she?"   6580
No hiding her identity:
"Fair sire," said Erec, "this lady

is my wife's mother." "Truthfully?
Her mother, is she?" "As you see."   6584
"Then I can say, with certainty,
no wonder, that, from such a tree,
the flower is so exquisite,
and the fruit, too, one plucks from it,   6588
so fair, and pleasing to the sense.
Knowing your Enide's excellence,
it seems but right and natural,
the mother being so beautiful,   6592
the father, too, so fair a knight.
True gold, this girl; no counterfeit,
false to her lineage. In worth
she bears resemblance to them both."   6596
He spoke; concluded thus his speech;
was silent. Then he asked that each
be seated. He was not gainsaid,
but readily they all obeyed.   6600
    As for Enide, her joy was great.
Too long she had been separate
from her dear kin. Much time had passed
since she had seen her parents last.   6604
Joy now suffused her, and increased,
more and more happy and more pleased
she grew, and showed it all she could;
for more she felt, there where she stood,   6608
than she had power to express.
    I wish to say no more of this:
for now my heart is urging me
to speak of the fair company   6612
from many lands, from diverse places.
Kings and counts of many races,
Normans, Bretons, Scots, and all,

and folk of England and Cornwall,   6616
great lords from Wales down to Anjou,
from Germany and from Poitou.
There was no noble chevalier,
or lady, sage and debonair,   6620
none brave, rich, or magnificent,
who did not gather there at Nantes,
assembled by the king's decree.
Hear me! Hear of this company!   6624
Hear how among great courtiers,
great lords, how before the hour of terce
there, by King Arthur their seignior,
four hundred knights were dubbed, and more,   6628
and all were sons of counts and kings.
Bestowed on them were precious things:
Three horses had each scion and prince,
and, for the sake of elegance,   6632
three pairs of suits. Oh, these were not
mere cloaks of serge, that each man got,
cheap rabbit fur, or flimsy wool;
but Arthur, great and powerful   6636
gave gifts that truly suit a knight.
Ermine, these robes, and rich samite,
and flowered silk, and bright striped vair,
and stiff gold braid that edged the fur.   6640
    Great Alexander, conqueror
of all the earth, a warrior
magnificent and generous,
would seem, here, parsimonious.   6644
Caesar, of great Rome emperor,
and all the kings of ancient lore
in songs and in chansons de geste,
could not have laid out such a feast   6648

as Arthur gave, with such display
on Erec's coronation day.
Caesar, with all his opulence
would not have dared so much expense,   6652
nor—I will say it in all candor—
would that proud wonder, Alexander.
Mantles and cloaks lay spread for all
to help themselves, throughout the hall;   6656
garments were taken from the chests,
and each could take what he liked best,
with no objections. And, inside,
laid on a rug, there were supplied   6660
big bushels—thirty, easily.
White sterlings held they, currency
in common use since Merlin's day,
and known throughout all Brittany;   6664
now, each could carry what he might
to his own place, that Christmas night.
      That Christmas night, when terce had struck,
they were assembled, all the folk;   6668
Erec, enraptured, saw approach
that moment's joy that meant so much.
No man has mouth or tongue to say
—however great his artistry—   6672
one third, one fourth, one fifth the grandeur
of this event, its joy, its splendor.
What folly are my poor attempts
to tell you the magnificence   6676
of that great day! But tell I must.
And so compelled, I do my best
to offer, with some wit and sense
something of its great elegance.   6680
In the great hall, a radiant sight—

two thrones of ivory, fresh and white
and beautiful. In style and height
they were a match; whatever wight   6684
designed them, knew his trade, for sure.
Skilled and ingenious art they were:
in length and breadth a perfect pair,
as in their ornament, so fair.   6688
Study them both in great detail
from every side, at last you'd fail
to make distinction of one throne
and tell it from the other one.   6692
No wooden pieces would you see,
but gold, and purest ivory,
sculpted with great precision. Couched
in two throne legs, two leopards crouched;   6696
two other legs formed crocodiles.
A knight, Sir Bruianz of the Isles
had brought them to the royal pair.
    Arthur, upon one splendid chair,   6700
make Erec take the other one.
Watered silk vestments he had on.
Hear what the story says to us
of Erec's robe: Macrobius   6704
wrote of it with great artistry.
From him I draw authority,
by him am taught. Believe that I
do not exaggerate or lie.   6708
Macrobius, in his famous book
teaches me, as I read and look,
what workmanship was there, what fine
figures were in that robe's design.   6712
Four fairies, with great mastery,
had woven it. The first fairy

had there portrayed Geometry,
how, with each figure, each degree,   6716
she calculates the measurement
of all the heavens' and earth's extent
and misses nothing. Depth, and height,
length, width, she gets exactly right,   6720
and calculates so perfectly
how vast and deep is all the sea;
so the world's measured and is known.
Thus the first fairy's work was done.   6724
The second labored to portray
Arithmetic, as skillfully;
how, with her quick intelligence,
she gives Old Time his measurements,   6728
the days and hours. And one might see
how all the waters of the sea
are counted, drop by drop; her hand
sorts through them, sorts the grains of sand,   6732
and counts the stars up, one by one.
Who better speaks the truth? She's known,
in the world's forests, all the leaves.
No number tricks her, or deceives;   6736
she never fails in her intent
when on her task her mind is bent.
Thus was Arithmetic portrayed.
Now the third fairy had displayed   6740
Music, in whom all joys accord
in harmony, with no discord,
in harp or viol or joyous rote.
Marvelous was this work; it showed   6744
all pastimes in their merriment,
and every singing instrument.
The fourth fay's work was best of all.

Shown there was the most wonderful 6748
of all the arts, Astronomy.
Through her, what marvels we can see!
Counsel she takes from stars, each one,
holds conference with the moon and sun; 6752
only these Presences are source
of all that she must do, perforce.
Good counselors, they, and sure to tell
all she requires, superbly well, 6756
and what has been, and what will be
shines in their faces, verily —
no false appearances to see!
Woven thus was Astronomy. 6760
This was the work that was portrayed
in Erec's robe; and it was made
with gold thread, fine and delicate.
And the fur lining under it 6764
came from a beast most strange and rare;
its head stark white and singular,
a neck that is mulberry-black
and violet, a crimson back 6768
and blackish belly. This strange beast,
native to India and the East,
goes by the name of *barbiolet*.
Nothing but [spices] will it eat, 6772
fresh clove and bark of cinnamon.
What can I say, what can my tongue
speak, of this cloak's magnificence?
Splendid it was, at all events, 6776
and fair. Among its tassels hung
four stones; two amethysts, that swung
and flashed, with blue and violet lights;
the other two were chrysolites, 6780

golden; and all in gold were set.
   Enide, it now appears, has yet
to make her entrance. Arthur says,
noticing how Enide delays,   6784
Gawain must go and fetch Enide.
Gawain sets off. He makes good speed,
no loiterer, he, at such commands!
With him is good King Cadiolanz,   6788
and Galloway, of such largess;
Guivret le Petit, too, no less,
leads them; and Yder, son of Nut,
with other barons, follows suit.   6792
More than a thousand men, they lead
Queen Guinevere and Dame Enide.
Great knights upon these ladies wait;
so many, they could decimate   6796
a host of foes. The queen had spent
great pains, great art, on this event,
dressing Enide in splendid stuffs.
Now Sir Gawain the courteous   6800
was at her side, and Galloway,
of great largess, most gallantly
led her as well. He held her dear,
for Erec was his nephew. Here   6804
comes this great progress, to the hall!
Now Arthur hastens, and withal
generously, and with kingly grace
greets her, and leads her to her place   6808
beside Erec, for he intends
much honor to her. Now he sends
for two great crowns out of his store.
Massive, full of fine gold, they are.   6812
When his command is given out,

quickly these splendid crowns are brought
glowing with garnets, to the king.
Each has four stones, all sparkling.   6816
However radiant the moon
with wide white light, these stones, each one,
the dullest, shows a light so clear
it darkens and eclipses her.   6820
Glowing and singing light, it's thrown,
breaking on palace wall and throne,
dazzling, just for an instant, all
the subjects gathered in the hall;   6824
Arthur, too, blinded by the sight,
stunned, still rejoices in its light.
  Two maidens take the first bright crown;
two barons take the other one.   6828
Arthur now bids forth all the priors,
bishops and abbots, worthy sires,
to the new king's anointing, since
this is the law for Christian prince.   6832
Now they come forth, the prelates all,
white-haired and young, at Arthur's call;
abbots and bishops and clerks; their sort
is much in evidence at court.   6836
The sage and saintly bishop of Nantes,
himself, performed the sacrament
for the new king; performed the rite
as was most holy, fair and right,   6840
placing on Erec's head the crown.
Arthur had now brought forth and shown
a scepter, lovely beyond peer.
Let me recount its beauties; hear!   6844
Limpid and light and clear as glass,
formed from one emerald, green as grass,

huge as a fist, it was. Hear me!
Truth here I offer recklessly: 6848
No beast, of any form or size,
no man, no fish, no bird that flies,
no creature, feral, foul or fair,
lives, but had chiseled image there.   6852
King Arthur took it; marveled; and
placed it in King Erec's right hand,
offering it immediately.
Thus all was done as it should be.   6856
Then Queen Enide was also crowned.
    And now the bells for mass all sound.
To the main church they all repair;
in the cathedral, gathered there,   6860
they hear the service and the mass.
There, weeping in their happiness
you could have seen Tarsenesyde,
who was the mother of Enide;   6864
you could have seen old Licoranz
the father, weep at fate and chance,
which can be good. Ecstatic pair!
As they approached in joy and prayer,   6868
out came a joyous band, who bore
relics and treasures, precious store
—Bible and censer and crucifix—
few churches, abbeys, bishoprics   6872
can boast of such. Beloved saints' bones
in reliquaries, splendid ones—
this was the shining, sacred store
that met the nobles at the door.   6876
There was no lack of songs and chants.
Never have been more kings and counts
and dukes assembled at a mass.

So great the press, so dense the mass,   6880
the church was bursting out the doors.
There was no room for oafs and boors,
but only ladies and great knights.
Outside the door pressed many wights   6884
who could not enter for the mass.
   The service had been heard at last;
now to the castle all repaired.
There all was readied and prepared,   6888
the tables placed and cloths spread out—
five hundred tables, I've no doubt.
But now I do not want to tell
a tale you'll think impossible,   6892
that row on row these tables all
were set up in the palace hall.
There were five halls, all crowded thus,
and one would find it arduous   6896
to make his way and force some space.
And at each table there was place
set for a king; a duke; a count.
One hundred chevaliers, by count,   6900
set in each group and shared the spread.
A thousand knights passed round the bread;
a thousand, wine; a thousand, food;
their robes were ermine, fresh and good.   6904
Such diverse dishes they all ate!
If I do not enumerate,
I could give an account, you know.
To other tasks I now must go   6908
[than talking of their drink or meat;
there was no lack of things to eat.
Each had, according to his wish,
all, in great plenty, of each dish.   6912

When the feast ended joyfully,
King Arthur left, in company
with nobles, kings and dukes and counts.
It would be hard to keep accounts   6916
of noble folk and menial
who were there at the festival.
Hard, too, to keep account of all
the silver, steeds, arms; wonderful   6920
delicate silks and finery;
great, Arthur's generosity,
he so loved Erec, held him dear.
The tale that I have told ends here.]   6924

Notes to the Poem

16 "Une molt bele conjointure" in the Guiot MS. *Conjointure* means a juncture, a joining action, and the phrase is the first, and the plainest, of Chrétien's indications of his conscious craftsmanship. Carpentry and masonry are obviously implied as metaphors for his art. Chrétien intends a seamless joining of the *sen*, or thesis of the work, with the *matière*, or the material, the narrative. Jean Frappier, who defines *conjointure* as "coherent narrative" or "well-ordered story," adds: " 'Conjointure' ensures the internal coherence and unity of the subject, establishes a link between the continuity of events and the depiction of characters, and may even aim for a latent architectonic structure in the romance" (*Chrétien de Troyes: The Man and His Work*, trans. Raymond J. Cormier [Athens: Ohio University Press, 1982], 45).

22–24 The Breton *conteurs* of whom Chrétien speaks so disparagingly were the descendants of Britons who, over generations, left what is now England, fleeing the Anglo-Saxon invaders, and settled in what is now Brittany. They and their descendants often became bilingual, and while mingling with the French, still communicated with their own close relatives, the Welsh and Cornish peoples. When Arthurian legends were developed and disseminated in Wales, Breton minstrels (or *conteurs*, storytellers) imported them to the mainland.

As Roger Sherman Loomis writes, "A class of wandering minstrels, with histrionic talents, found that this novel material captivated barons and their ladies, not only in Brittany but wherever French was understood. More and more they adapted the fantastic tales to French tastes, manners, and standards of rationality, costumed their characters according to the latest mode, and introduced all the pageantry of chivalry." This audience had wearied of the epics of Charlemagne and took up with great enthusiasm these Celtic tales of love, marvels, and derring-do. See Loomis, *The*

Development of Arthurian Romance (New York: W. W. Norton, 1963), 33–34.

40–42   W. W. Comfort, in the notes to his translation of Chrétien's romances, quotes Wendelin Foerster's comment that "we frequently read in the romances of a hunt at Easter." Comfort points to one such hunt in the romance *Fergus* (c. 1230), where Perceval kills the animal, although "there is no mention of the ceremony of the bestowal of the kiss" (Chrétien de Troyes, *Arthurian Romances* [New York: E. P. Dutton, Everyman's Library, 1914; reprinted 1970], 361).

43   In the early romances, Sir Gawain is the knight whose reputation for *courtoisie*—and for shrewdness and perception in all its matters—is greatest. In late Arthurian romance, such as Malory, he is far more at the mercy of his weaknesses and passions.

50   In the Welsh fourteenth-century analogue, *Geraint Son of Erbin,* the lady receives not a kiss, but the head of the slain stag. See *The Mabinogion,* trans. Gwyn Jones and Thomas Jones (New York: E. P. Dutton, Everyman's Library, 1949; reprinted 1974), 241, 245–46.

84   A palfrey was the riding horse of the upper classes. It is sometimes referred to as a lady's mount, but there are numerous accounts of gentlemen of the period riding palfreys. See, for instance, Margaret Wade LaBarge's delightful and informative *Medieval Travellers* (New York: W. W. Norton, 1983), esp. 35–39; and Urban Ticknor Holmes, Jr.'s, classic *Daily Living in the Twelfth Century* (Madison: University of Wisconsin Press, 1952), 52.

88   Comfort remarks that "Chrétien nowhere gives any description of the nature of the Round Table. With him, it is an institution. Layamon in *Brut* and Wace in *Le Roman de Brut* are more specific in their accounts of this remarkable piece of furniture. From their descriptions and from other sources in Welsh and Irish literature, it is reasonable to suppose that the Round Table had a place in primitive Celtic folklore" (*Arthurian Romances,* 361).

98–107   The destrier was the powerful and very expensive mount used by the knight in combat. When it was not being ridden, a squire or a knight, riding a palfrey or some other lighter horse, would lead the charger at his right, controlling it with the reins in his right hand (*a destre,* whence the name). For Erec to ride a destrier though he bears no arms or armor makes him appear to be displaying himself a bit excessively, with youthful pride.

Erec's attire, too, may be a sign of his youthful pride in his role and reputation. (Ermine could only be worn by those of noble rank.) However, as Margaret Wade LaBarge succinctly writes, "Medieval society had a strong sense of 'estate,' a belief that each person had a special place in society—usually through birth, sometimes by function—which he was bound to uphold and make clear to those around him. Thus it was the pleasant duty of the rich and powerful to wear fine clothes and jewelry, to ride a spirited horse, to set a generous table, and to scatter largess among the less fortunate" (*Medieval Travellers*, xii). Such behavior is evident throughout this romance.

128 *Chaceor,* or "hunter," in the original. Holmes comments that "the best horses and mules at this time were supposedly the Spanish breed. (This was not the same as Arabian.) The Spanish horse was sturdy, fairly low, with flowing mane and tail" (*Daily Living,* 310).

152 Dwarfs were frequently associated with evil. See the Introduction (14, 14n, and 17 above).

164 "Young girl," or "maiden." The word was pronounced *putzelle* in Old French.

213 The word *vassal* had several meanings. Here it is a form of address appropriate to a young nobleman, either a comrade or someone with whom one must exchange the courtesies of rank. It could also refer to any noble, valiant young man, as well as a noble or knight who had sworn fealty to a lord.

349 *Chastel,* in the original, ordinarily means a walled town, not a separate fortification or building. In places I have translated it as "town" or "city."

356–58 As Carleton W. Carroll remarks, "Hunting with hawks was one of the most important pastimes of the medieval nobility. . . . The term 'hawk' could refer to either the long-winged falcons or the short-winged birds known commonly today as hawks, and might include either sex. When one wishes to distinguish between the sexes, 'falcon' is used for the female of all long-winged hawks, and 'tercel' for the male (but the male sparrow-hawk is called a 'musket' " (in William W. Kibler, trans., Chrétien de Troyes, *Arthurian Romances* [New York: Penguin Books, 1991], 505). Hunting birds varied greatly in size, from the relatively small sparrow hawk to the goshawk ("about six times the size of the sparrow-hawk," Carroll remarks) and the very large gyrfalcon.

Hawks molt—that is, they shed and grow new plumage every year, except for the first year of life. A sorrel hawk is a young bird that has not yet shed its juvenile plumage. Carroll calls the plumage of such a goshawk "reddish"; translating the same passage, Comfort (*Arthurian Romances*) calls it "yellow"; and D. D. R. Owen (trans., Chrétien de Troyes, *Arthurian Romances* [New York: E. P. Dutton, 1987]) calls it "tawny." *Mewed* (line 357; French *mué,* from Old French *muer,* "to change") is an older word for *molted.* The word has a time-honored association with falconry; a place where these hunting birds are maintained in captivity is traditionally called a *mews.*

379   A vavasor (from Latin *vassus vassorum*) was the vassal of a vassal rather than of a king. Comfort remarks that "the vavasors are spoken of with respect in the Old French romances, as being of honorable character, though not of high birth" (*Arthurian Romances,* 361).

406   The discerning reader will notice that, whereas the hero is described as being just under twenty-five years of age (line 94), the girl's age is not discussed at all. It is probably safe to assume that she is in her mid-teens. Holmes, in discussing the education and rearing of young people of some rank, remarks: "The boys were usually considered of age at twenty-one, but it might be earlier. Girls, of course, were ready for husbands at fourteen or fifteen years of age, and occasionally they were married off even earlier" (*Daily Living,* 178).

407–9   Enide wore a chemise, or undergarment, with a long, full, pleated skirt, and over that the customary *chainse.* A *chainse* was a long white dress with very tight sleeves and was made of linen or hemp. Fashionable ladies of this period wore a *chainse* of linen that trailed to the ground, with fine tight sleeves that extended to the wrist (sometimes so tight they had to be sewn up each time the dress was worn). Over the *chainse* came a tunic (a *bliaut* or *cote*) with long, full sleeves; the *chainse* might show a bit above the neck of the *bliaut* and below the *bliaut*'s hem. Poorer women wore a somewhat shorter-sleeved *chainse* and a *bliaut* whose sleeves reached to the wrists. For a fuller description, see Holmes, *Daily Living,* 163–64; he remarks that "it was . . . possible to move about in the *chainse* alone [i.e., with no *bliaut* over it], but that was considered insufficient." See also Kibler, *Arthurian Romances,* 504 (s.v. "Tunic").

427   Legends of Iseult, Tristan, and Mark were current at the time,

made popular by Breton *conteurs*. The Norman poet Béroul and the Anglo-Norman Thomas, contemporaries of Chrétien, wrote accounts of the Tristan story, which survive in fragments. Chrétien says that he also wrote a version of the story, but it does not survive.

520   Comfort notes (*Arthurian Romances*, 362) that in *Geraint Son of Erbin*, the host explains that he had wrongfully deprived his nephew of his possessions, and that in revenge the nephew had later taken all his property, including an earldom and the town in which they live. (See *The Mabinogion*, 235–36.)

554   "Chivalry" is here meant in the sense of "cavalry," mounted men at arms.

718   The hauberk (*hauberc*) was a shirt of mail reaching to the knees. Holmes describes it (based on his inspection of fifteenth-century mail coats, since twelfth-century mail coats no longer exist) as

woven from a series of round metal links, usually of steel, each link locking with the six or more surrounding ones. The result was a springy mesh, weighing sixty pounds or so, which broke the force of a blow by its resilience. It also retarded the blow from a sharp edge. It was not so satisfactory against an arrow well shot. . . . A lining made of felted animal hair was sewn into the *hauberc*. . . . [It] had a short sleeve, like that of civil dress. This meant that the forearm was not protected. When the knight was going into battle, long mailed gloves or mittens could be laced to the sleeves of the *hauberc*. A *sarcot* of handsome cloth was often worn over the *hauberc*, giving a natty appearance. The *hauberc* had a hood, called a *coiffe*, which slipped over the head. This was, naturally, of the same material as the *hauberc* itself. Often this *coiffe* was covered with a helmet.   (*Daily Living*, 167–68)

Holmes also quotes *Erec and Enide*—lines 2626–58 in this translation—to show how a knight arms himself with these accoutrements (167); Prince Erec, of course, had finer arms than most knights. For variations on the style of the *hauberc* and other features of the chevalier's arms, see 167–172.

720   The ventail was made of linked meshes and covered the lower part of the face. It was attached to the *coiffe* on each side of the neck and

protected the throat. (See Comfort, *Arthurian Romances,* 362; Kibler, *Arthurian Romances,* 504; and Owen, *Arthurian Romances,* 498.)

794 Sergeants (*serjants, sergenz*) were professional soldiers of the bourgeois or peasant class in the service of a nobleman or clergyman. Holmes remarks that it was sometimes difficult to tell a sergeant from a knight. Often, however, a sergeant wore armor that was a generation out of date, "probably consisting still of heavy canvas with rings or leather plates sewn on it" (*Daily Living,* 172–73).

873 Holmes describes a shield of the period as being commonly "of linden wood boards, nailed side by side and cemented further with the help of casein glue. These boards were covered on the exterior with heavy hide," which was painted and sometimes varnished as well. The shield might be silver, red, blue, yellow, or some other bright color, or it might have a design, though heraldry was only beginning to be in evidence (*Daily Living,* 171–72).

1170 Comfort notes: "The 'loges,' so often mentioned in old French romances, were either window-balconies or architectural points of vantage commanding some pleasing prospect. The conventional translation in the old English romances is 'bower' " (*Arthurian Romances,* 362).

1321–22 The original is "sires seroiz de Roadan, / qui fu fez des le tans Adan" (Roques, lines 1319–20); "You will be lord of Roadan, which was built as early as the time of Adam."

1329 *Vair* here refers to the spotted gray and white fur of the northern gray squirrel. This highly prized fur, like ermine, could only be worn by the nobility. Holmes remarks that "the white fur of the squirrel formed the background, and pieces of grey were sewn onto this in ten or twelve rows or 'tongues' " (*Daily Living,* 162).

1339 Scarlet (or crimson or red) referred in color symbolism to joy and magnificence and to love. For the gown, Chrétien uses the word *robe.* Roques says that this word refers to an ensemble formed of two garments (chemise and *chainse, bliaut* and mantle; see his edition, 260–61). René Louis uses the modern French *robe* ("dress" or "gown") in his French prose translation (*Erec et Enide* [Paris: Champion, 1954], 35); Comfort, in his version, uses "dress" (*Arthurian Romances,* 18). It seems likely that Erec was thinking of a *bliaut* (a full-sleeved overgarment), and perhaps a matching mantle, to wear over a *chainse* (Enide's own or a better one).

1376   *Vair,* when used to describe the coat of a horse, meant dapple gray. Such horses were thought very elegant and were highly prized. (Elsewhere I have translated *vair* as "dappled" (1394) or "dapple gray" (1371), partly to provide a convenient explanation in the text and partly to cope with the demands of meter and rhyme.)

1417   *Amie* means "(woman) friend," "sweetheart," "lady love," or "girlfriend." *Ami* is, of course, the corresponding masculine form.

1570–1606   Cf. notes to lines 408–10 and 1339. The outfit Enide receives appears to be an ensemble: she has an ermine dress and a mantle with matching ermine lining.

1603   I have used the word *ell,* supplied by most dictionaries, to translate Chrétien's word *aune.* Both were units of measure. Kibler says that an *aune* was equivalent to about four feet (*Arthurian Romances,* 502). The word *ell* varied in meaning in different countries. In England it signified 45 inches; in Flanders, 27 inches, or three-quarters of a yard.

1809   *Escarlate* (from medieval Latin *scarlatum*) was a silk or wool of fine quality. The color varied greatly.

1884–1961   Owen comments, "Like the list of Arthur's knights [when Enide is presented at court, lines 1671–1706 above], this enumeration of his vassals contains names and allusions that are obscure to us. Some may have been gleaned from tales of Celtic provenance circulating during Chrétien's day" (*Arthurian Romances,* 501).

1899   The Guiot MS has "li sires de l'Isle Noire" (Roques, line 1897), i.e., the Black Isle. Since other MSS (including B.N. MS 1450, from the same tradition as the Guiot) have *Voirre,* or "Glass," and the place described is traditionally the Glass Isle, I have assumed that *Noire* is a scribal error. (See also Glossary, below, s.v. Glass Isle.)

1976   This passage has been much discussed and has baffled some scholars. Comfort says in a note to his translation: "With what seems to us mistaken taste, Chrétien frequently thus delays mentioning the name of his leading characters. The father and mother of Enide remain anonymous until the end of this poem" (*Arthurian Romances,* 363). Luttrell finds Chrétien's withholding of Enide's name a "mystery," inadequately explained by Chrétien's sources (*The Creation,* 169). Carroll remarks: "Much has been written concerning *retardatio,* the technique of postponing the revelation of a character's name until long after that character's first appearance" (*Erec and Enide*, 318). It is possible that Chrétien was experimenting with *retardatio* or mocking it. Also, naming may symbolize the recognition and acceptance of Enide's identity, as an individual and as an important member of the community. My own supposition, fairly literal, is that Enide, heretofore known to the court as Erec's mysterious lady love, is now very properly addressed by her baptismal name at her wedding by the archbishop of Canterbury, who blesses her.

1993–94 *Viele*, in the original, may be an ancient viol (such as that played by an ass sculpted on the outer wall of Chartres Cathedral; he holds it against his shoulder), or it may be a *vielle à roue*, or hurdy-gurdy. The hurdy-gurdy referred to here is not a boxlike barrel organ, but a lutelike instrument; the musician turns a crank attached to a wheel that plucks or scrapes the strings.

1996 A carol was originally a round dance; the dancers would sing as they circled.

2077 Roques remarks that the manuscript tradition here is "most confused," and that the scribes appear not to have known whether they were dealing with the names of people or of places (220). "Tenebroc" is Edinburgh, and in MS B.N. 1450, "Evroïc," i.e., York, appears instead of "Erec." My translation follows MS B.N. 794 (the Guiot), although MS B.N. 1450 does give a clearer reading: the chevaliers will choose either Edinburgh or York as the site for the tourney, and Gawain on one side makes surety, and Melis and Meliadoc on the other side.

2081 The *défi* was the formal challenge to combat made by one knight to another.

2123, 2128 The name Orguelleus means "proud one."

2213 Solomon was the embodiment of wisdom for people of the Middle Ages.

2215–16 Alexander the Great was especially revered in Chrétien's time for his legendary largess, or generosity. (See also lines 6641–44, 6654.)

2391 A *brach* (diminutive *brachet*) was a female hound; a *lévrier* is a greyhound.

2685–93 Nobles did not commonly ride alone. Cf. Chrétien's *Yvain*, in which a knight describes himself as traveling "seus come paisanz" ("alone, like a peasant"; line 174 in Mario Roques's edition [Paris:

Champion, 1960]). LaBarge also comments that people of rank traveled with a large retinue (*Medieval Travellers,* 16).

2926　A knight is often described as holding his lance "sor le fautre." Both Roques, in the glossary to his edition (254), and Holmes, in his description of a knight's furnishings (*Daily Living,* 170–71), describe the *fautre* as a rug or padded cloth laid on the horse's saddle. "A lance on the *fautre,*" writes Holmes, "would mean that the hand holding the weapon is resting on the saddlecloth, or that the butt of the lance is reposing there." (See also lines 4427, 5749.)

3124　Roques defines these "fromages de gaïn" as cheeses made after mowing time, of richer milk from better nourished cows (255).

3391–92　In the original Enide says to the count: "Je vos voldroie ja sentir / an un lit certes nu a nu" (Roques, 3390–91). *Nu a nu* (literally, "nude to nude") was a common expression, used often with far less physical immediacy; it meant "directly," "without interference," "without intermediary."

3523　Roques comments that horseshoe nails were bigger and heavier in Chrétien's period and would thus show more plainly in the hoofprint, if the horse had been at all recently shod, than they would for a modern horse. These nails afforded greater stability on wet or icy terrain. Since shoeing methods varied from locality to locality, the hoofprint of a stranger's horse could often be identified easily by anyone inclined to do a little sleuthing (222–23).

3594　These would be French acres, about one and a half times the size of English ones.

3682　*Lices* were mounting blocks, enabling a knight in heavy armor to get up on his horse.

3801　Terce was the third of the seven canonical hours—roughly, 9:00 A.M. None was the fifth canonical hour, at about 3 P.M. (or the ninth hour of the day).

3850　Loomis believes that "Irois" (Irish) is a scribal error for "li rois" (the king). (See *Arthurian Tradition and Chrétien de Troyes* [New York: Columbia University Press, 1949], 145.) Although his comments are somewhat conjectural, they do explain why the text states that a Welsh king is served by Irish vassals.

4243   Owen remarks in his note to this line: "It being the eve of Sunday, no meat was eaten" (*Arthurian Romances*, 303).

4331–33   The bracketed lines are from MS B.N. 1450; they make more consistent sense than those in the Guiot MS, which reads "Or est Erec an grant peril" ("Now Erec is in great peril"). This line would have to be an aside by the narrator, interrupting the lady's speech. Although Erec's situation is perilous, it seems more likely that the lady is still speaking of her unfortunate lover, as MS B.N. 1450 suggests: "Or est de mort an grant peril" ("Now he is in great peril of death"). See Roques, 226; also Louis's translation, viii and 113.

4374   Here Comfort remarks that "in the French epic poems and romances of adventure alike it is customary for giants and all manner of rustic boors to carry clubs, the arms of knighthood being inappropriate for such ignoble creatures" (*Arthurian Romances*, 364). As we have already seen, whips and scourges were also popular weapons for oafs and boors.

4500–4508   The Guiot MS leaves out the short passage in which Cadoc of Tabriol tells his name. I have supplied those lines from MS B.N. 1450, which come after Guiot line 4488. See Roques's edition, 226–27; also Louis's translation, viii–ix, 118.

4619–51   Comfort calls this passage "an excellent example of an Old French lament for the dead. Such a wail was known in Old French as a 'regret,' a word which has lost its specific meaning in English" (*Arthurian Romances*, 364).

5093–94, 5175–5207   Comfort here notes, "Many examples will be met of women skilled in the practice of medicine and surgery" (*Arthurian Romances*, 364). It is true that women practiced medicine in the Middle Ages; some of them, in a fairly humble capacity, were midwives and dispensers of infusions and potions for the common people, but others attended universities and became physicians.

5303–7   Owen (*Arthurian Romances*, 504) remarks, "The palfrey presented to Enide is clearly no ordinary animal. Although nothing similar appears in *Geraint*, it may be compared with the parti-colored beasts found in Celtic mythology. Enide's earlier mount given her by her cousin may likewise have had supernatural origins (see Loomis, *Arthurian Tradition and Chrétien de Troyes*, pp. 105–8)."

6357–58   "Symphonia" and *"armonie"* (or "armonia") were both names for the hurdy-gurdy; the symphonia was the larger instrument.

6439   This line has puzzled scholars. The original is "de li poist l'en oiseler." Roques comments that although the line appears in all MSS and is clearly Chrétien's, "its meaning is very uncertain" (230). Either, as Roques suggests, one feels a birdlike, soaring exultation at seeing such joy as the queen felt or, as Gaston Paris suggested, Guinevere herself is ready to fly into the air for very joy. I have attempted to express a sentiment something like the latter, which seems to me probable in this context.

6709   Macrobius was a fifth-century Neoplatonic philosopher and Latin grammarian, best known for his *Saturnalia,* an academic symposium, and for a commentary on Cicero's *Somnium Scipionis* (Dream of Scipio) in Cicero's *De Republica.* Both the *Somnium* and Macrobius's *Commentary* are works of profundity and charm, offering a tour of the universe and admonishing the reader not to fear mortality. Macrobius's *Commentary* enjoyed great popularity in the Middle Ages. It is referred to by Jean de Meun, Gower, and Chaucer (who used it to beautiful effect in his *Parlement of Foules*); no doubt it is the work Chrétien had in mind.

6771   This animal has never been identified as a real creature, although Carroll notes that it has been "plausibly identified by Glyn Burgess and John Curry (1989) as the multicoloured douc langur monkey of the Asian subcontinent" (*Arthurian Romances,* 508). Burgess and Curry go to some trouble to describe this animal in detail—its coloring and eating habits —and make a case for its being the rare creature Chrétien describes (" 'Si ont berbioletes non' [*Erec et Enide,* l. 6739]," *French Studies* 43 [1989]: 129–39).

6772   The Guiot MS has for this line *poissons* ("fishes"); other manuscripts have *especes* ("spices"). Roques thinks *poissons* makes fair sense (234), so he does not alter the line. For me, *especes* makes far more consistent sense, and in view of Chrétien's fastidious and careful artistry, I have selected this reading.

6909–24   The text of the Guiot MS (and three related MSS) ends abruptly at our line 6908. I have added sixteen lines that appear at the end of the work in three other MSS—B.N. 375, B.N. 1420, and B.N. 1450—to give what seems a more fitting conclusion.

Glossary of Names and Places

About some of the figures Chrétien mentions in *Erec and Enide* little is known today. The more obscure figures may well be drawn from Celtic legends and tales popular in Chrétien's time but lost to us. The reader who wishes more information on Arthurian knights mentioned in this romance may find much of interest in Loomis, *Arthurian Tradition and Chrétien de Troyes;* Flutre, *Table des noms propres;* and West's two indexes (see Suggestions for Further Reading, above).

Absalom 2212. The son of King David in the Old Testament (2 Samuel 13–19). In the Middle Ages he was considered a type of ideal masculine beauty. Cf. Chaucer's *Miller's Tale,* where a very handsome (and foppish) young man has the name Absolon.

Aguiflez 1920. King of Scotland; guest at the wedding of Erec and Enide. In Wace's *Brut* his kingdom is Anguisseaus; in Geoffrey of Monmouth he is king of Albany, a land near Scotland. (See Loomis, 478; West, *Verse Romances,* 8.)

Amauguins 322, 1696. A king; knight of the Round Table.

Antipodes 1944. A mythical people in Libya, described by the seventh-century writer Isidore of Seville. According to Isidore, they were dwarfs whose feet pointed backward, with eight toes to each foot.

Ares 1510. A king; father of Cortz.

Arthur 32 (first mention). The legendary king of Britain. The earliest reference to him appears in the Welsh poem *Goddodin* (c. 600). Legends of Arthur are generally believed to have originated in Welsh mythology and folklore. Geoffrey of Monmouth (c. 1135) presents him as the conqueror of Western Europe; Wace (1155) makes him a chivalric hero. In Chrétien he is portrayed as a great king and a promulgator of the chivalric ideal; he is occasionally impulsive or whimsical, or (in *Perceval*) weak and in need of aid from his vassals. Chivalric tradition names him as one of the Nine Worthies, among whom he, Charlemagne, and Godfrey de Boullion are the three exemplars of Christian chivalry.

Aumarie 2363. Almería, a city and seaport in southern Spain, in Andalusía. An ancient city known in Roman times (as Urci or Portus Magnus), it received its present name from the Moors and was under Moorish domination for most of the Middle Ages.

Avalon 1907. The magical island ruled by Guingamars. According to Loomis (478), the name derives from Welsh "ynis Avallach" (Isle of Avallach) and later might have been influenced by Breton place-names Bothavalon and Avaelon. The Welsh isle takes its name from Avallach, father of Modron, the goddess who was the original of Morgan la Fée. Morgan, Guingamars' *amie,* is often represented as the lady of the island. See also *Romanic Review* 29 (1938): 176f., and *PMLA* 56 (1941): 920.

Bans 1925. King of Ganieret. This name may well be a scribal corruption of Bran, derived from the Welsh King Bran (Loomis, 478).

Bedoiers 1703. The constable. A similar figure appears in Wace, Bedoier the *bouteiller,* or cupbearer, to King Arthur.

Bilis 1943, 1947, 1952, 1953. King of the Antipodes, a dwarf people; guest at the wedding of Erec and Enide.

Bliant 1946, 1948. The giant brother of King Bilis of the Antipodes. According to Loomis (479), the name Bliant is a variant of Brien, a Breton name, substituted for Welsh Bran, a legendary giant. See also Loomis, 242–43 and 435, and *PMLA* 56 (1941): 921–24.

Blioberis 1688. Knight of the Round Table. Loomis states that this name (and its many variations) is a corruption of Bleheris, the name of a famous *conteur,* and was mistakenly applied to a knight. (Loomis, 479; see also West, *Verse Romances,* 20–21.)

Brandigant 5370. The castle of King Evrain. Its name may derive from King Bran, with Bran taken for a place name, to which an ending was then added by analogy to Car(a)digan (Loomis, 479).

Brangein 2022. Handmaiden of Queen Iseult. In the legend she agrees to lie with King Mark, secretly taking Iseult's place on the royal wedding night. In some versions of the story the lovers later plot Brangein's murder, since she alone knows of the substitution.

Branles of Colchester 1887. A guest at the wedding of Erec and Enide.

Bravains 1705. A knight of the Round Table.

Bruianz of the Isles 6698. In the later prose romances, this knight engages in forays against Lancelot and against Arthur, and is the lover of the beautiful fay Esclarmonde, whom Loomis regards as a double of Morgan la Fée (see *Arthurian Tradition*, 157). In the romance *Escanor*, this fay bestows upon Bruianz a chamber decorated with scenes from the legend of Troy, an interesting parallel with the carving of the Aeneas story in ivory and gold on the saddlebows of Enide's palfrey (See also West, *Verse Romances*, 27–28.)

Cadiolanz 319, 6788. Caedwalla, historic king of northern Wales (d. 634). Here he is a vassal of Arthur's, called to council in the dispute over the ritual of the stag and the kiss.

Cadoc de Tabriol 4500, 4530, 4559. The knight saved by Erec from the two vicious giants.

Cadret 1922. Son of Aguiflez, king of Scotland; guest at the wedding of Erec and Enide.

Caloain. The obsessively vain count who attempts to seduce Enide, first by persuasion and then by threats to kill the wounded Erec. Although this figure is not mentioned by name in the Guiot MS, MS B.N. 1450 names him once, at line 3122 of that MS, when Erec and Enide are found by the kindly squire in the forest; I have supplied his name at line 6461. Loomis believes that the name (with its variant Galoain) is a form of Gawain (or Gauvain) (483).

Cappadocia 1923. An ancient region of Asia Minor, located in what is now eastern central Turkey.

Caradué Briebraz 1689. A knight of the Round Table.

Caraduel 5260. Probably modern Carlisle (Roques ed., 243).

Cardigan 32, 253, 288, 1030, 1086, 1501. A city in Wales (spelled both Caradigan and Quaradigan in the MS). Loomis says that this name was originally Norman, not Welsh (29, 75).

Carnant 2261. A castle; probably Caerwent in Monmouthshire (Roques ed., 236; Loomis, 481).

Caverons de Roberdic 1691. A knight of the Round Table.

Cortz 1510. Son of King Ares. Origin unknown (Loomis, 491; there the name is listed as Tor or Torz, following MS B.N. 1450).

David   1911. King of Tintagel; guest at the wedding of Erec and Enide. The name is taken from the Biblical King David (Loomis, 482; West, *Prose Romances,* 93).

Do   1697, 2176. Father of Gilflez.

Dodins the Wild   1680. *Li Sauvages* in the Old French.

Enide   406 (first appearance), 1983 (first named). The heroine of this work; Erec's *amie* and wife. The source of her name is unknown.

Erec   21 (first mention). The hero of this work; a knight of the Round Table, son of King Lac of Estre-Gales (southern Wales). Loomis says that the immediate origin of the name is Guerec, which is also the ancestor of Geraint, the hero's name in the Welsh analogues (482).

Estre-Gales   1827; rendered "Outer Wales" at 3865. Realm of King Lac, Erec's father. According to Loomis (482), the *D* of *Destregales* was mistaken, by Chrétien or an earlier source of his, for the preposition *de* (with the *e* elided before a vowel). *Destregales* was French for "right Wales," i.e., southern Wales, and thus corresponds to Welsh Deheubarth, "right part," applied to southern Wales.

Estre Posterne   1904. Finistère; the ancestral home of Greslemeuf. In MS B.N. 1450 it is called *Fine Posterne,* which Loomis believes is a popular form of the name Finistère (483).

Evrain   5387 (first mention). King of the castle of Brandigan.

Fernaguz   5759. The hero of a French chanson de geste.

Galegantin   1706. A Welsh knight of the Round Table. His name may be a corruption of Galvagin, or Gauvain, i.e., Gawain (Loomis, 483; see also West, *Verse Romances,* 66).

Galeriez   1695. Younger brother of Gawain. In Malory he is Gaheris.

Galez li Chaus   1696. A knight of the Round Table.

Galloway   6789, 6801. Erec's uncle; king of Galloway in Scotland.

Ganieret   1925. The kingdom ruled by Bans.

Garraz   1915. King of Cork; guest at the wedding of Erec and Enide.

Gaudeluz   1681. A knight of the Round Table.

Gaudin of the Mountain   2173. Knight vanquished by Gawain at the tournament at Tenebroc.

Gawain   43 (first mention). Son of King Lot; Arthur's nephew. In many stories he is the best of Arthur's knights, famed for his perfect chivalry and *courtoisie* in the early romances. He retains that reputation in the fourteenth-century Middle English masterpiece *Sir Gawain and the Green Knight;* in Malory his character shows corruption.

Gilflez   321, 1697, 2176. Son of Do; a knight of the Round Table and participant in the tournament at Tenebroc.

Glass Isle   1899. Domain of Moloas. In Welsh legend it has associations with Anwyn, the abode of the Celtic gods, a Welsh Elysium. Through scribal error the name Isle de Voirre (itself a false etymology of the name Glastonbury, a town in Somerset; see Loomis, 218–20) was corrupted to Isle de Gorre, the kingdom to which, in Chrétien's *Lancelot,* Meleageant abducts Guinevere. In *Erec* (Guiot MS), reference to the Isle Noirre is also surely a scribal error.

Glodoalan   1954. A dwarf king; guest at the wedding of Erec and Enide.

Godegrains   1895. A count; guest at the wedding of Erec and Enide.

Gonemanz de Goort   1675. A knight of the Round Table.

Greslemeuf d'Estre Posterne   1904. Vassal of Arthur and brother of Guingamars; guest at the wedding of Erec and Enide.

Grihalo   1955. A dwarf king; guest at the wedding of Erec and Enide.

Gringalet   3949, 4071. Sir Gawain's horse, which figures in many Arthurian tales. Loomis believes the name derives from either Old Welsh *guin-colet,* "white-hardy," or *Keincaled,* "handsome-hardy" (485).

Guincel   2172. A participant in the tourney at Tenebroc.

Guinevere   81 (first mention). Arthur's queen. She is famous, in other romances, for her adulterous love affair with Lancelot. Her name is derived from Welsh *guin-hwyfar,* "white phantom."

Guingamars   1906. Lord of the Isle of Avalon; brother of Greslemeuf and lover of Morgan la Fée; guest at the wedding of Erec and Enide.

Guivret   3852 (first mention). A dwarf king. His character is based on Welsh dwarfs Beli and Guidolyn, but the name is probably Breton (Loomis, 485).

Handsome Coward   1676. *Biax Coarz* in the Old French. A knight of the Round Table.

Iseult   427, 2021. Irish wife of King Mark of Cornwall; lover of Tristan in the celebrated legend of the two adulterous lovers.

Kay   321 (first mention). Seneschal of King Arthur; a medieval seneschal administered justice, oversaw the domestic affairs of his lord's estate, and represented his lord in court. In Arthurian tradition Kay is famous for his hasty bad temper, harsh mockery, and contentious dealings with others, as here in lines 3940–4061.

Lac   21 (first mention). Father of Erec; king of Estre-Gales, or southern Wales. The name is from Welsh *lluch,* or "lake"; Loomis believes his name goes back ultimately to the Irish sun-god Lug (486).

Laluth   349 (first appearance), 6226 (first named). The town where Enide and her parents live before her presentation at Arthur's court and marriage to Erec.

Lancelot   1674. Distinguished knight of the Round Table; in other romances, the lover of Guinevere.

Lavinia of Laurentum   5871. The daughter of Latinus; she is the second wife of Aeneas, the hero of Virgil's *Aeneid* and of the Old French *Eneas.*

Licoranz   378 (first appearance), 6865 (first named). The vavasor of Laluth; father of Enide.

Limors   4659 (first appearance), 4701 (place named), 4931 (count named). The estate of Count Oringle; the name also designates the count. This is the nobleman who forcibly marries Enide, believing Erec dead. His name may originally have meant *li mors,* or "the dead man"; in other words, he was, as Loomis writes, Death personified (486, 162–68).

Loholz   1700. Son of King Arthur; a knight of the Round Table.

Lot   1705. A king; Arthur's brother-in-law and the father of Gawain and Galeriez. His name, like King Lac's, derives from Welsh *lluch* or *lloch* (lake) and ultimately, Loomis believes, from the Irish sun-god Lug (487).

Lucan   1511. *Bouteiller,* or cupbearer, at Arthur's court.

Maboagrain   5877 (first appearance), 6112 (first named). Nephew of King Evrain; vanquished and freed by Erec in the Joy of the Court.

Maudiz the Wise   1679. *Le Sage* in the Old French. A knight of the Round Table.

Mean-and-Ugly Bold   1677. *Le Lez Hardiz* in the Old French. A knight of the Round Table.

Meliadoc   2078. The knight who leads one side in the tourney at Tenebroc.

Melianz des Liz   1678. A knight of the Round Table.

Melic   2078. A knight who participates in the tourney at Tenebroc.

Menagormon 1889. Lord of Eglimon; guest at the wedding of Erec and Enide.

Merlin 6663. The celebrated mage, counselor of Uther Pendragon and then of his son, Arthur. Merlin, by his magic, enabled Uther to lie with Queen Ygerne; thus Arthur was engendered. He planted in stone the sword which Arthur drew out to prove his right to the throne. In Robert de Boron's *Merlin,* in the romance *Claris,* and elsewhere, Merlin is the creator of the Round Table; in *Brut* and other Arthurian lore, Arthur creates it. For other details of the Merlin legend see West, *Verse Romances,* 115, and *Prose Romances,* 125; Loomis, 61–68, and his *Development of Arthurian Romance,* 124–30.

Moloas 1897. Lord of the Isle of Glass; guest at the wedding of Erec and Enide.

Montrevel 1325, 1835. A castle owned by King Lac; given to Enide's parents by Erec and Lac.

Morgan la Fée 1909, 2360, 4202, 4203. Arthur's sister; a famed enchantress. In much medieval lore she has a sinister and lascivious reputation. Her history is convoluted; Loomis believes she took over the Welsh traditions of the river-goddess Modron and the Irish traditions of the lamia and prophetess Morrigan (488).

Morholt 1244. Uncle of Iseult; Tristan killed him when sent to collect tribute from Morholt for his uncle, King Mark. The battle took place on an island that later versions of the story identify as Saint-Samson.

Nantes 6523, 6556, 6622, 6837. Ancient city in Britanny, on the estuary of the Loire. Traditionally the residence of the rulers of Brittany; seat of the dukes of Brittany in the Middle Ages and later.

Nut 1045, 1210, 6791. Father of Yder, the knight with the dwarf and proud *pucelle,* whom Erec vanquishes at Laluth and sends to Arthur's court. The corresponding Welsh figure is Nudd. This personage probably is descended, etymologically and mythologically, from the old British god Nodens or Nodons (Loomis, 488).

Opiniax 5759. King of Babylon in a chanson de geste now lost (Roques, 242).

Orguelleus de la Lande 2123. A participant in the tourney at Tenebroc.

Oringle The count of Limors. *See* Limors.

Perceval 1508. A Welsh knight of the Round Table; the subject of Chrétien's last romance and an important figure in Arthurian tradition, because he is the Grail knight. The corresponding Welsh figure is Peredur.

Pointurie 5088 (first mention), 5166 (first named). The castle of Guivret's sisters.

Quarrois 5259. A castle belonging to King Arthur.

Quenedic 1692. A king. Origin unknown (Loomis, 489).

Quex d'Estraus 1695. Probably a double of Sir Kay. Estraus is not explained (Loomis, 486).

Quintareus 1693. A knight of the Round Table.

Quirions 1935. The old king of Orcel; guest at the wedding of Erec and Enide.

Quoi 1922. Son of Aguiflez, king of Scotland; guest at the wedding of Erec and Enide.

Randuraz 2130. Son of the Vielle (the Old Dame) de Tergalo; a participant in the tourney at Tenebroc.

Red City, king of the 2140. A participant in the tourney at Tenebroc.

Roadan 1321, 1836. A castle of King Lac's, given to Enide's parents by Erec and Lac; possibly Rudlan in northern Wales (Roques, 243).

Roberdic See Caverons.

Sagremors 1701, 2177, 2184, 2196. A knight of the Round Table; a participant in the tourney at Tenebroc. His name is possibly derived from the word for "sycamore," though for unexplained reasons. He is often given the epithet *le Dezreez*, meaning "fierce" or "unruly," because of his impetuous nature (West, *Verse Romances*, 143).

Saint-Samson 1245. Island where Tristan defeated Morholt in combat; probably the island of that name in the Scilly Islands (Loomis, 490).

Tarsenesyde 405 (first appearance), 6863 (first named). Enide's mother; wife of the vavasor Licoranz of Laluth.

Taulas 1697. A knight of the Round Table.

Tenebroc 2077, 2085. Modern Edinburgh.

Tergalo 2131. A place-name associated with the Vielle (the Old Dame) who is Randuraz's mother. Not identified (Loomis, 491).

Thibaut li Esclavons 5757. Comfort remarks (365) that this knight, frequently mentioned in the epic poems, was a Saracen king, the first husband of Guiborc, who later married the Christian hero Guillaume d'Orange.

Tintagel 1911, 6490, 6499. A town where Arthur held court; a well-known castle on the coast of Cornwall.

Traverain 1893. A count; guest at the wedding of Erec and Enide. His estate might be Terweren, the residence of the dukes of Brabant (Roques ed., 244).

Tristan 1244, probably 1687. Lover of Queen Iseult in the celebrated legend. The name is derived from Welsh Trystan or Drystan, from Pictish Drustan, a king who reigned c. 780 (Loomis, 491); it later came to have associations with sorrow (*tristesse*) in love.

Tristan who never laughed 1687. A knight of the Round Table. Almost certainly a double of the famous unhappy lover.

Troyes 11. Ancient city on the Seine, 97 miles (165 km) south-southeast of Paris; formerly the residence of the counts of Champagne. See Introduction, pp. 6–7.

Uther Pendragon 1771. A king; father of Arthur. He engendered Arthur when, by Merlin's arrangement, he visited the beautiful Ygraine disguised as her husband, whom he had killed. His name means "Chief of Dragons."

Vale Perilous 2361. A haunt of Morgan la Fée's.

Vienne 5942. Ancient city on the Rhône, of Roman origin, located 17 miles (28 km) south of Lyon. In Chrétien's time it was part of the Holy Roman Empire.

Yder, son of Nut 146 (first appearance), 1045 (first named). Knight who, with his dwarf and haughty *amie*, insults Guinevere and Erec. Vanquished by Erec in a joust at Laluth and sent to Arthur's court to do homage, he becomes one of Arthur's knights. Chrétien probably intended to differentiate the three Yders (Ydier is a variant) who appear in this work, although the Welsh tales feature only one Edern, the son of Nudd, associated with King Arthur (Loomis, 491).

Ydiers 317. A king; called to council by Arthur after quarrels have begun over the ritual of the kiss and the stag hunt.

Ydiers of the Mount Dolorous 1694. A knight of the Round Table. He does not appear in MS B.N. 1450.

Yvain de Cavaliot   2176. A knight of the Round Table. Referred to simply as Yvain in the Guiot MS, he is given this title in MS B.N. 1450. His name is a corruption of Owein Cyveilioc, the name of a celebrated contemporary of Chrétien's who ruled over Cyveilioc. He was a distinguished poet, and was evidently on friendly terms with Henry II (Loomis, 492).

Yvain the Bastard   1686. *Li Avoutre* in the Old French. A knight of the Round Table; half-brother of Yvain the Valiant (*li Preuz*).

Yvain the Valiant   1685. *Li Preuz* in the Old French. The famous knight of the Round Table, celebrated in a later romance by Chrétien as the knight with the lion. Here he is a participant in the tourney at Tenebroc. Yvain is a Breton form of the Welsh name Owein; Owein was the historic son of Urien, who was a famous prince of the north Britons of the late sixth century. Although Chrétien distinguishes between the three Yvains, there is reason to believe that they are one and the same, as in the case of the three Yders (Loomis, 492).

Designer: Janet Wood
Compositor: A-R Editions, Inc.
Text: Garamond
Display: Erbar, Cochin Italic
Printer: Thomson-Shore, Inc.
Binder: Thomson-Shore, Inc.